The dog playground on
New York's East River Waterfront
Esplanade is 4,750 square feet.
Discover more creative
revelations in this book...

**50 design questions answered**

ARUP

# Foreword: Sir John Sorrell

I believe we are at the dawn of a new age – where nations, cities and businesses are increasingly turning to creativity and design to achieve growth and success.

It is in this context that Arup works, designing at the leading edge with a social purpose and helping shape a better world. These principles are at the core of Arup. And nowhere is that better demonstrated than in the projects featured in this Design Book.

For Arup, design is about the impact on people's lives. Over the past year it has continued to design, build, engineer, research and inspire buildings and urban landscapes that generate healthier, safer environments with great amenities and stunning architecture.

This book shows the diversity of Arup's work. It showcases large-scale projects such as HS1, which became the foundation of the London 2012 Olympic and Paralympic Games, and smaller ones that are transforming people's lives in different parts of the world, from Ireland, where Arup is helping to tackle flooding, to a project in China bringing farming skills into a city.

As well as new projects, this book covers the evolution of some of the world's most iconic structures, such as the Sydney Opera House and the Lloyd's Building in London, two relationships Arup continues to uphold.

Global issues such as climate change and population growth are explored along with research studies that could lead to solutions to address these problems. For Arup, which I believe is among the world's most creative organisations, the desire to find answers to difficult questions sets it apart and is what makes it so different and special. It is therefore apt that this design book is themed around questions that challenge our thinking and encourage us to see the world through a different lens.

**Sir John Sorrell, CBE**
UK Business Ambassador, Creative Industries

# Contents

If you change
the view of the
'inside-out'
building, will
you spoil it?

Few buildings are as distinctive as the one that houses Lloyd's of London, the specialist insurance market. When replacement windows were needed for the 'inside-out' building, the brief was clear: retain the iconic 1986 building's distinctive glazing, but update it, giving occupants more light and better views.

The original bespoke 'sparkle' glass, with its raised pimples, offered privacy and a light-diffusing effect to the interior, but it also made the offices dark and obscured views of the city.

We returned 30 years after working on the original build and devised a sustainable refurbishment solution. Instead of changing, recreating or replacing all of the sparkle glass, original panels were partnered with new, clear glazing within the original frames.

Now the sparkle glass look is still there, but the new clear glass sections have been placed logically to let in more light and allow occupants to see out. A total of 1,182 window bays have been reglazed, using a third of the original panes, a sustainable solution that saved on money and materials.

As the building is occupied, construction workers busied themselves at night like the shoemaker's elves, moving desks, circumnavigating fitted kitchen units and IT equipment, then returning every last paper clip to its place by morning.

**Project name:** Lloyd's Cloudless
**Designed for:** Lloyd's of London
**Designed with:** Rogers Stirk Harbour + Partners

"The brief from Lloyd's was to improve the quantity and quality of light entering the building and at the same time enlarge the external views. The stunning result gave us views out of the building but maintained the integrity of the building we love"

Darren Cox, Facilities Planning Manager, Lloyd's Property Services

**What can
a dragonfly
teach us
about design?**

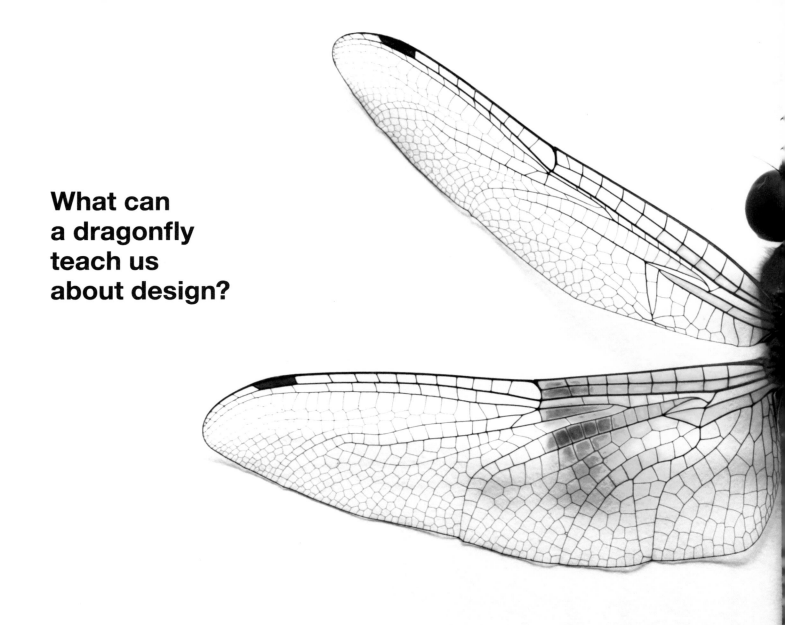

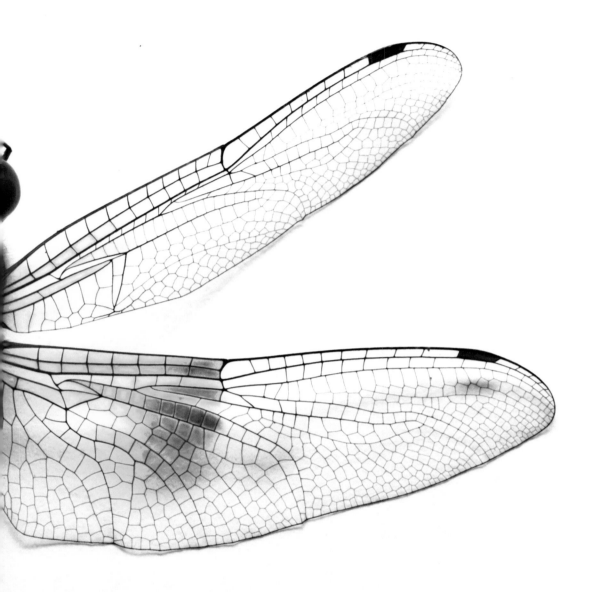

Designers can learn a lot from nature. It takes millions of years for highly developed animals and insects to evolve, which are precisely adapted to be the best they can be.

One example of this is the dragonfly, whose wing has evolved so that its complex cellular structure automatically distorts when it is simply pushed up and down.

We wanted to understand if we could learn from this and, by doing so, whether it would help us produce simpler yet similarly adaptive structures in the built environment.

Maria Mingallon, a senior structural engineer, studied dragonfly wings as part of her master's degree at the Architectural Association in London.

Through her research Maria observed a parallel between a dragonfly's wing and the structure of buildings. The wings are made of layers of a thin material called chitin that can be configured to be either flexible or rigid to support flight. It's a remarkably efficient system that gives maximum effect by using minimum effort.

Understanding how the wing can be both flexible and stiff could help us design structures that deal better with seismic forces, or reduce vibration in buildings where lighter materials have been used.

Biomimicry – taking lessons from nature – can inform and enhance design, as we continue to strive to make each structure smarter and more efficient than the last.

Maria created a digital reproduction of the wing to analyse it and identify vibrations otherwise invisible to the human eye. Further investigation of the type and distribution of joints along the wing could improve the way we design moving parts for dynamic structures.

We still don't know where the answers will take us, but investing in research always takes us on a journey of discovery.

**Project name:** The Dragonfly Wing and Digital Computation
**Designed with:** Sakthivel Ramaswamy, KRR Engineering

# How easy is it to camouflage a building?

Among the fauna, flora and foliage, visitors to Australia's Cairns Botanic Gardens may also stumble across a man-made structure. The mirrored façade of the visitor centre has been designed to merge with its green surroundings.

The vast foldaway, full-height walls and a cantilevered roof over the open-air, wall-less amphitheatre are designed to bring the outside in.

The result is a visitor centre that quite literally reflects the tropical rainforest.

**Project name:** Cairns Botanic Gardens Visitor Centre
**Designed for:** Cairns Regional Council
**Designed with:** Charles Wright Architects

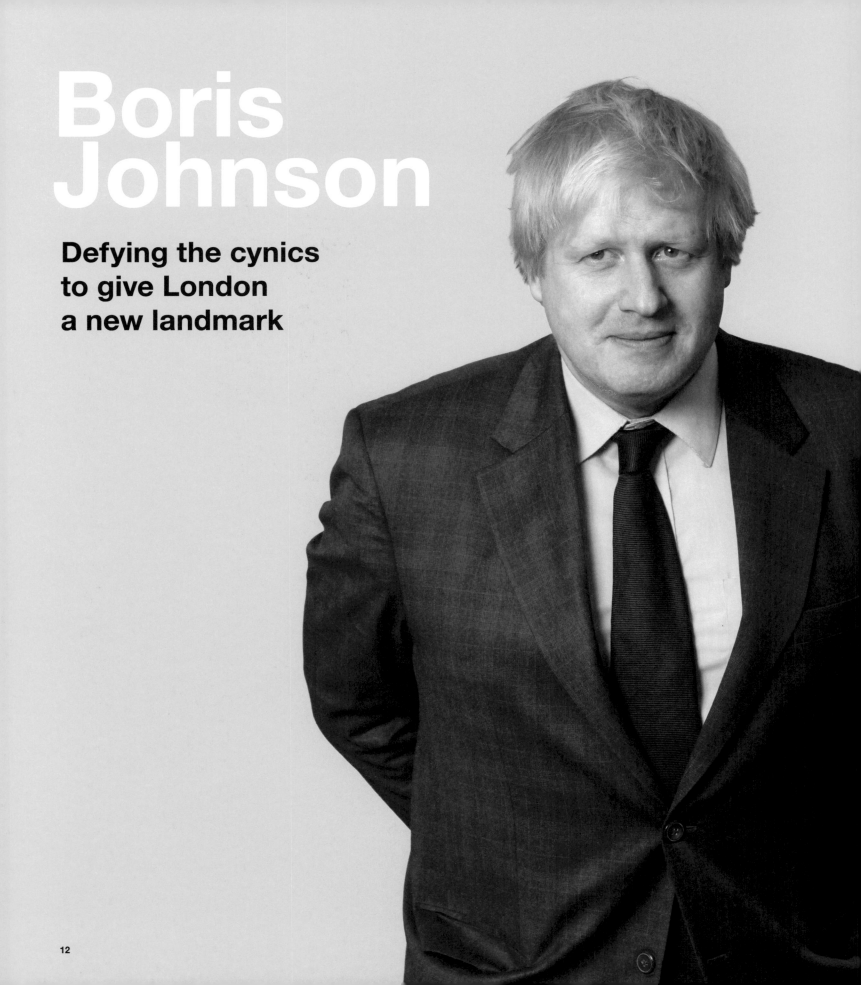

# Boris Johnson

## Defying the cynics to give London a new landmark

# "Orbit is a lasting reminder of the great talent, endurance and world firsts that represented the Games"

The London 2012 Olympic and Paralympic Games were a golden opportunity to stage a global event that would continue to benefit the city's future generations through urban transformations.

With about three years to go before the opening ceremony, it was clear that the sports venues and arenas of the Olympic Park were going to be constructed on time and would suit their functions perfectly. They are all magnificent buildings in their own right and were imagined, designed and built by teams of people over several years. But I felt that the park needed something extra, a landmark structure – outside the core Olympic facilities, which would provoke debate and excite the park's visitors for generations to come. This was the genesis of the sculpture and observation tower that became known as the ArcelorMittal Orbit and is the UK's largest piece of public art.

Some people thought that parachuting such a hugely ambitious structure into a large, organised and complex project was madness. Our team had to prove these doubters wrong and, at the same time, provide East London with an icon that would play a significant role in the legacy of the park.

Since this project couldn't be publicly funded, we found a sponsor in steel giant ArcelorMittal and launched a competition that attracted some of the best designers in the world. Anish Kapoor's winning concept, which combined architecture and structural engineering, represented the scale and ambition of the Olympic Games. It was also achievable within the time frame ahead of the Games, but we had just 27 months to complete Orbit.

Failure to meet the turnaround time would have been personally and politically embarrassing for me, but failure was not an option. So we turned the construction process on its head. In a normal project, the design process goes through a number of stages, progressively becoming more detailed and better defined. But Arup, as principal designer, had to hit the ground running from day one.

Everything that would usually be done in a measured sequence had to run simultaneously. Flexibility and a nimbleness to adapt to the unique challenges of the project over its 2-year gestation were essential. Perhaps most important of all was an ability to manage the more than 90 designers, engineers, planners and technical specialists, who spent the equivalent of 14.5 man-years from conception to completion working on the project in time for the opening ceremony.

Orbit was a truly Olympian project. Once we agreed that we were going to build it, we let nothing stand in our way until completion. I imagine this is a little like the mindset of an Olympic champion – they don't ever believe that they are going to fail.

Orbit was a huge talking point during the Games. But no matter how many times you see pictures of it in the press or on television, there is no substitute for seeing it up close and in person. The public were drawn to it and that desire to experience Orbit will continue as the Stratford site transforms into the Queen Elizabeth Olympic Park.

In some ways, Orbit's journey mirrors that of the Games. People doubted whether both could be pulled off and were sceptical of the legacy they would leave. But Orbit became a huge part of the skyline that symbolised London during the Games. And it is a lasting reminder not only of the Olympic spirit of cooperation, but also the great talent, endurance and world firsts that represented the Games.

**Boris Johnson** is the Mayor of London

(The ArcelorMittal Orbit, part of the legacy of London 2012, can be spotted on page 19)

How do you
create an urban
landscape?

The process of creating an urban landscape for London's East End began in 1989, when we proposed connecting the Channel Tunnel to London via a station in Stratford, East London. Our strategy was to cause one of the biggest urban regeneration projects in the UK, which ended up encompassing the London 2012 Olympic and Paralympic Games. Stratford's journey is ongoing.

At first, ours was a lone voice challenging the UK Government and British Rail's plans to run High Speed 1 (the old Channel Tunnel Rail Link) tracks through South London, terminating at Waterloo. After years of painstaking research we built a compelling case.

Our route ran north of the Thames, through Stratford and into St Pancras. The link provided easy access between London's East End and the heart of the capital. This alignment would catalyse the multibillion-pound regeneration of East London and parts of Kent in south-east England. The Secretary of State for the Environment at the time was an early convert. With his support, we convinced the UK government that the 'Arup Alignment' could trigger transformative growth.

With the rail line secured, we developed plans to regenerate the redundant rail yards at Stratford, creating a new metropolitan centre for London.

The rail link provided the infrastructure behind the London 2012 bid that won over the International Olympic Committee delegates. The pre-existing regeneration plans promised a lasting, sustainable legacy after the Games.

The urban transformation is continuing to help revitalise one of the most deprived areas of London.

It might have been two decades down the line from our original plans, but London 2012 was just the beginning.

**109km**
of track make up the £5.8bn High Speed 1 rail link

# Stratford's regeneration journey

### 1991: The 'Arup Alignment'

The government selects the 'Arup Alignment' for the £5.8bn High Speed 1 (HS1) rail link, with its predicted £10bn economic benefits for Stratford. We set up London and Continental Railways, which wins the concession to build, own and operate the 109km high-speed railway and own the British share of Eurostar. More than 1,600 of our staff work on the project. HS1 is opened by the Queen in 2007.

### 2002: London's Olympic bid

In 2002 the UK government asks us to study the costs and benefits of hosting the Olympic Games in Stratford. In 2003, it decides to bid for the Games after our study shows the economic gains will outweigh expenditure. London wins the bid in 2005.

### 2005: The Stratford site

While excavating the route beneath what is now Stratford City, we use the soil from tunnelling to lift the land out of a flood plain. In doing so, we create valuable new land for development. It means that not only does the proposed site promise to bring economic prosperity, but related work in the area increases its value.

### 2007: Creating Stratford City

Stratford is London's first new metropolitan centre since the 1950s, including Europe's largest single retail development, offices, hotels and open spaces. Our specialists work across every aspect from wind engineering to energy.

## How Charles Darwin lit up an Olympic stadium

Solving a problem with the lighting in London 2012's venues came down to the survival of the fittest.

A year before the Games, broadcast images from test events showed too much flicker. This was because today's super-slow-motion camera technology captures the flicker of lamps turning on and off 100 times a second. Our lighting experts created a genetic algorithm – an artificial intelligence that mimics Darwin's theory of natural selection – to create a solution. We often use such techniques in structural engineering but this was the first time we'd used them on a lighting project.

The 500 lights in the Olympic Stadium were separated into three time phases to smooth out the flicker. Success depended on which lights were used for which phase. Our software used the algorithm to simulate millions of combinations, scoring each light in its different phase. The good combinations were kept, the bad thrown out and the average mixed together iteratively to form the fittest solution.

In three venues, including the Olympic Stadium, lights were repositioned to achieve a 60% reduction in 'flicker factor'. This technique saved roughly £500,000 compared with buying extra kit. Pin-sharp replay images of athletes straining every sinew were the result.

**35,000**
new homes are set
to be built by 2025
as part of the post-
Games regeneration

### 2012: The Games begin

We have an onsite office of 200 and more than 1,000 staff worldwide working on infrastructure and venues, designing and developing a site with a focus on legacy and sustainability. Our efforts on the site – including our stadium lighting project, opposite – facilitate a hugely successful Olympic Games, creating new usable, valuable land ready to be developed in the future.

### 2013: A legacy of growth

The Games are set to contribute an estimated:
£16.5bn to Britain's GDP between 2005 and 2017
354,000 man-years of employment

By 2025:
£22bn will have been invested
35,000 new homes and 100,000 jobs will be created*

Not a bad return on the original £500m of investment expected**

**Project name:** Channel Tunnel Rail Link, Stratford City, London Olympic and Paralympic Games, HDTV sport lighting
**Designed for:** UK Government, Greater London Authority
**Designed with:** Various

\* Source: London Borough of Newham, *Destination Newham. A new heart for London*
\*\* Source: Colin Buchanan and Partners Ltd in association with Volterra, *Economic Impact of High Speed 1*

Can you

# hear me California?

"The only thing better than this installation was playing the show" – Lou Reed's verdict on the recreation of one of his New York City Metal Machine Trio gigs in 3D sound.

The installation immerses the listener in the performance; they hear it from centre stage – just as Lou Reed did. It was conceived by a team of our acousticians, many of whom are also musicians, using SoundLab.

Our recording transported listeners back to the live show

To recreate the live experience of being right on stage at New York's Blender Theater performance of 'Creation of the Universe', we recorded the show using a number of techniques – including placing a 3D microphone behind Lou's head on stage and suspending several more above the audience.

The recordings were used in an exhibition at the University Art Museum at California State University, Long Beach, which allowed visitors to experience the gig first hand. The near-perfect audio recreation of the original performance was a completely visceral experience for visitors.

**Project name:** Lou Reed's Metal Machine Trio
**Designed for:** California State University
**Designed with:** Lou Reed

# Can buildings learn from a ship in a bottle?

It might seem like magic, but putting a ship inside a bottle is a mechanical puzzle that has been around for hundreds of years.

The puzzle is working out how something so large can fit through a relatively small hole and be reassembled inside. The principle was applied to the transformation of a late Art Deco power plant in Lansing, Michigan where it was important to keep its historical façade, but the inside needed to be completely rebuilt.

The endgame was taking the Great Depression-era building and making it fit for a 21st-century insurance company workforce.

As engineers, we don't take the easy option: we take the one that will achieve the vision. So, in the largely floorless tower of the old coal-fired plant more than 1,000 tonnes of the old steel framework were taken out through holes in the roof and new floorplates were created with almost 2,000 tonnes of new steel. This was dropped piece by piece through the roof – the same way the old

material was removed – and then reassembled inside to form new offices.

We reused and exposed existing structural elements, and maintained the volume of the turbine hall by suspending the new office space within. The historic refurbishment is linked to a new-build office building by an atrium. We had to carefully upgrade the glazing in the historic façade and find ways of linking the new office floors with the vast original windows.

It was worth the effort. The revitalised Accident Fund Insurance Building is such a popular architectural attraction that guided tours have been set up in response to visitor demand. This new design has brought some power back into a historic building.

**Project name:** Accident Fund Insurance Company Headquarters
**Designed for:** Accident Fund Insurance Company of America, Christman Capital Development Company
**Designed with:** HOK, Quinn Evans Architects

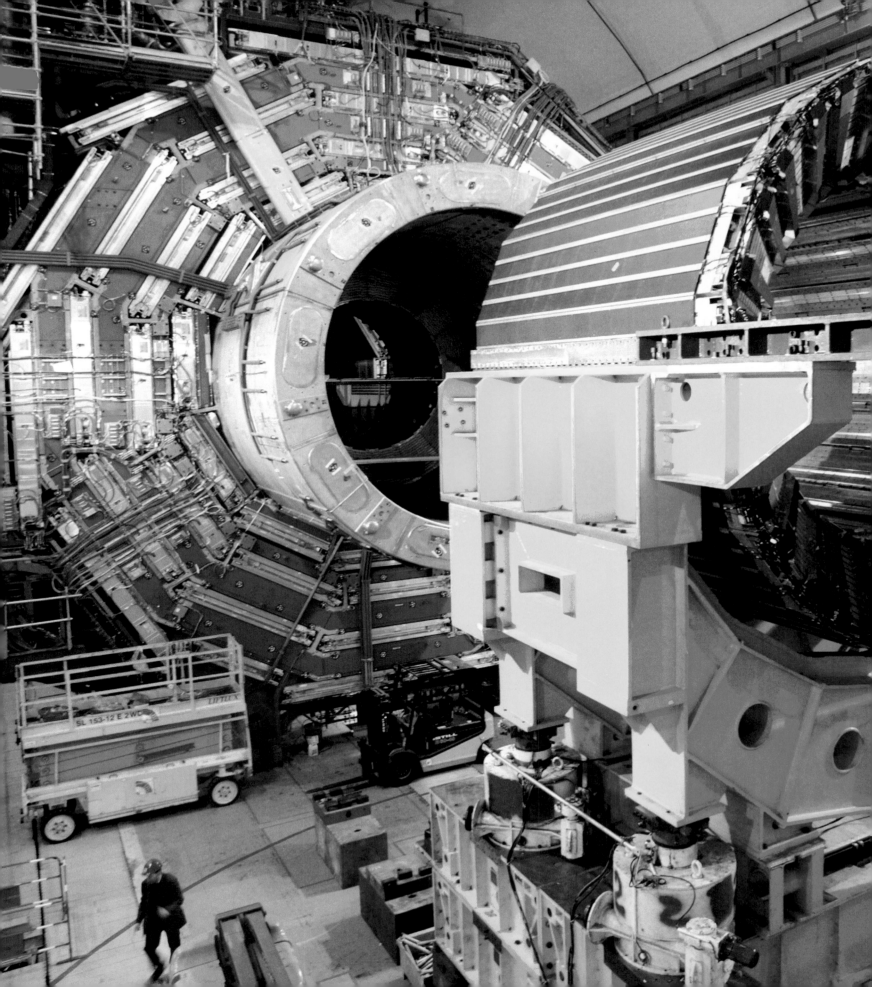

The Compact Muon Solenoid detector at the Large Hadron Collider shows the scale of the engineering challenge that would be faced

# How do you move 30,000 tonnes of steel without damaging our understanding of the universe?

Explaining something truly out of this world often requires a bit of help from something firmly grounded in the earth. Nowhere is that more true than in the case of the Higgs boson. Finding the 'God particle', using the Large Hadron Collider, was just the beginning of a journey.

What comes next is a deeper understanding of the universe. That will require continued research with the Large Hadron Collider, complemented by a new machine that could be a linear collider with two giant detectors. Alternating between them, these detectors would capture data from electron-positron collisions. Not only would they be highly complex, they would also be large, heavy and very fragile. And they would have to be positioned and moved with great care, since any jolts could affect their accuracy.

None of this makes it easy to move the equipment underground from the detector hall to maintenance garages. A rock-solid foundation would therefore be needed, so that when a detector is online, it is perfectly stable to detect and record collisions.

There are several potential sites for such a facility, CERN near Geneva being just one of them. For their feasibility studies our engineers had to verify the methods proposed for the lifting, transportation and precise positioning of the two 15,000-tonne detectors, which would need to be moved up to 10 times a year to an accuracy of 1mm – anything less would not be acceptable. We had to understand movement in the ground many layers below and on the slab the detectors will sit on and then apply that knowledge.

To do this, we used sophisticated 3D geological modelling to design the slab as well as the movement systems. And we also modelled the transportation tunnel and garage areas.

Our study proved the feasibility of the movement system and the suitability of the CERN site as a potential location for a new collider, and can be used as a basis for assessing the suitability of other locations.

And with that, we are helping the researchers in their efforts to achieve a better understanding of the universe.

**Project name:** Feasibility studies for a proposed Linear Collider
**Designed for:** The European Organization for Nuclear Research (CERN), Fermilab

What can we
learn about urban
sustainability
from a building?

The Crystal (left and right) showcases the future of the built environment – when climate change and renewable energy drive a shift to all-electric, smart buildings

When the Mayor of London put green enterprise at the heart of East London regeneration plans, The Crystal was held up as the showcase for what could be achieved.

The ethos behind the building was to create a show-stopping piece that illustrated the many ways in which buildings can reduce their impact on the environment. The result is the ultimate 'show and tell' building, which not only engages, inspires and teaches, but is housed in a crystalline shape that represents and delivers many aspects of sustainability.

A rooftop photovoltaic system that converts sunlight into electricity, a water treatment network that enables 90% water self-sufficiency and ground source heat pumps are just some of the sustainable elements of the building.

The Crystal points the way for the future of sustainable commercial developments in urban environments. The building neatly showcases many of the intelligent green design solutions that will help our cities forge a cleaner future.

**Project name:** The Crystal
**Designed for:** Siemens
**Designed with:** Pringle Brandon Architects, Wilkinson Eyre Architects, Turner & Townsend
**Awards:** The world's first double badged LEED Platinum, BREEAM Outstanding building

# What can business learn from consumers?

When time is money, there is much to learn from the consumer. Apps might have enhanced our daily lives, but business has been slow on the uptake – until now.

Arup Inspect has revolutionised the slow process of note taking and photography at site inspections.

The app now automatically locates you using GPS, and pulls together notes with the appropriate photography. It means that a process that used to take weeks – collating information, transcribing notes, pairing photography and remembering detail – is all at your fingertips.

**Project name:** Arup Inspect
**Designed with:** Fusion

# Elizabeth Farrelly

## Engineers and the poetics of space

# "This is today's great task: unifying technology and poetry in the interests of survival"

Who really designs buildings? Although both engineers and architects regard the mysterious activity we call 'design' as their territory, it is generally only architects who get to be the rock stars.

Throughout the modern era, architects have positioned themselves as the imagineers of the built environment, turning words into drawn spatial concepts. With one or two exceptions – notably the Spanish architect and engineer Santiago Calatrava – this has established a dualism, splitting the poetics of space (architecture) from its more prosaic technologies (engineering). In celebrity terms, at least, it has also put the poets on top.

Yet it is clear that such a split is illusory and unhelpful. It is as though the architect were writing the words of a poem, while the engineer supplied the sonnet structure. Ridiculous as it is, this dualism shapes our perceptions and our world.

Consider the Sydney Opera House. Two books that centre on the Opera House's story are Philip Drew's biography of its architect, Jørn Utzon and Peter Jones' biography of its engineer, Ove Arup. The books are virtually identical in size, weight and even in their blue-black colour.

Yet there is a tell-tale difference. The Utzon cover features the architect in his prime, clearly in control, pencil in hand, with the Opera House as a tiny inset image, bottom right. The Arup cover, by contrast, centres on the Opera House while the man himself is set below, back to camera. Arup's tonsure of white, wispy hair catches the light and his posture is slightly bowed, like an elderly sage giving obeisance.

Utzon and Arup were probably equally essential to reifying the masterwork, and the quality of their engagement equally imaginative. Yet on the building's designer label, the signature is unquestionably Utzon's.

Perhaps that's fine. Certainly, it is what it is. But as we move into the future, resolving this false dichotomy between poetry and technique may become a question of survival.

The Sydney Opera House is beloved across the world for neither its acoustics nor its structure, but for its beauty; the shimmer of light across its surfaces, the prehistoric heft of the concrete, the sheer effervescence of form, the foam at the meeting of two cultural oceans that produced it.

The post-modern world has taken this phenomenon and capitalised it. Steve Jobs turned Apple into a global behemoth not through superior functionality, but through the simple charisma of aesthetics – visual, aural and kinaesthetic. Suddenly, we are not just resigned to planned obsolescence in our consumer objects, but eager for it, so that we can trade up to our next and newest iteration. This is the power of seduction, not persuasion; working not through the mind but through the senses.

The next millennium, if we are to avoid catastrophe, must be the green millennium. Yet it is by now clear that humanity cannot self-discipline *en masse*. We cannot shift our own behaviours broadly enough or quickly enough to avert such catastrophe.

It is clearly time for the big guns. And the best, most dramatic and most reliable motivator of human behavioural change is, if you will forgive the word, beauty.

The world's star architects – such as Zaha Hadid and Frank Gehry – understand this quite as surely as Jobs did. Imagine, though, if any of them had harnessed that power not to profiteering, but to greening. Imagine if the forces of seduction, rather than mere persuasion – the forces of poetry, rather than science – were brought to bear in swinging the vast human *Titanic* around, from catastrophe to survival.

This is today's great task: unifying technology and poetry in the interests of survival. Making science sing. In many ways, engineers are the best-equipped professionals for the task.

**Elizabeth Farrelly** is a Sydney-based architecture critic and author

How does an
architectural
icon improve
with time?

The Sydney Opera House is one of the most famous buildings in the world and its history is inextricably linked with our own. Our founder, Ove Arup, was involved in the original design, which began in the 1950s, and our relationship continues to this day. We have unrivalled knowledge of the building and the peninsula on which it sits.

So when the Opera House needed to modernise the original plans to better understand the building, and to design any future changes, they came to us.

We worked with the original hand-drawn plans and drawings and also used the data from a laser scan of the interiors of the two main halls to generate a digital 3D model.

This helped us design the proposed works for the Venue Improvement Plan.

Several years on, we were appointed as part of the design team to improve vehicle and pedestrian access to the venue.

This project was designed in 3D and the building contractor has used the digital model extensively to plan and build the project, including testing plans for construction using computer-generated simulations.

The advent of digital modelling and ever-improving software means that works on buildings, such as the Sydney Opera House, can be easily planned and implemented while the venue can operate without disruption.  >

The Sydney Opera House receives 8.2 million visitors each year

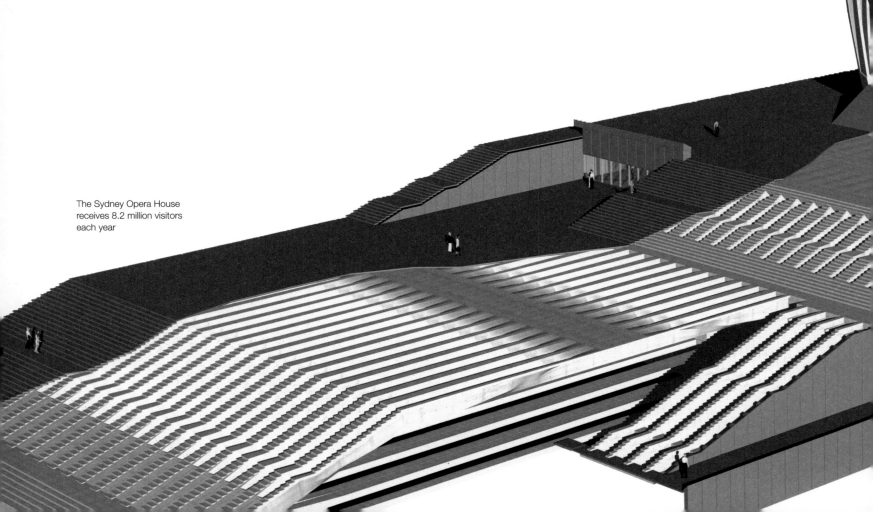

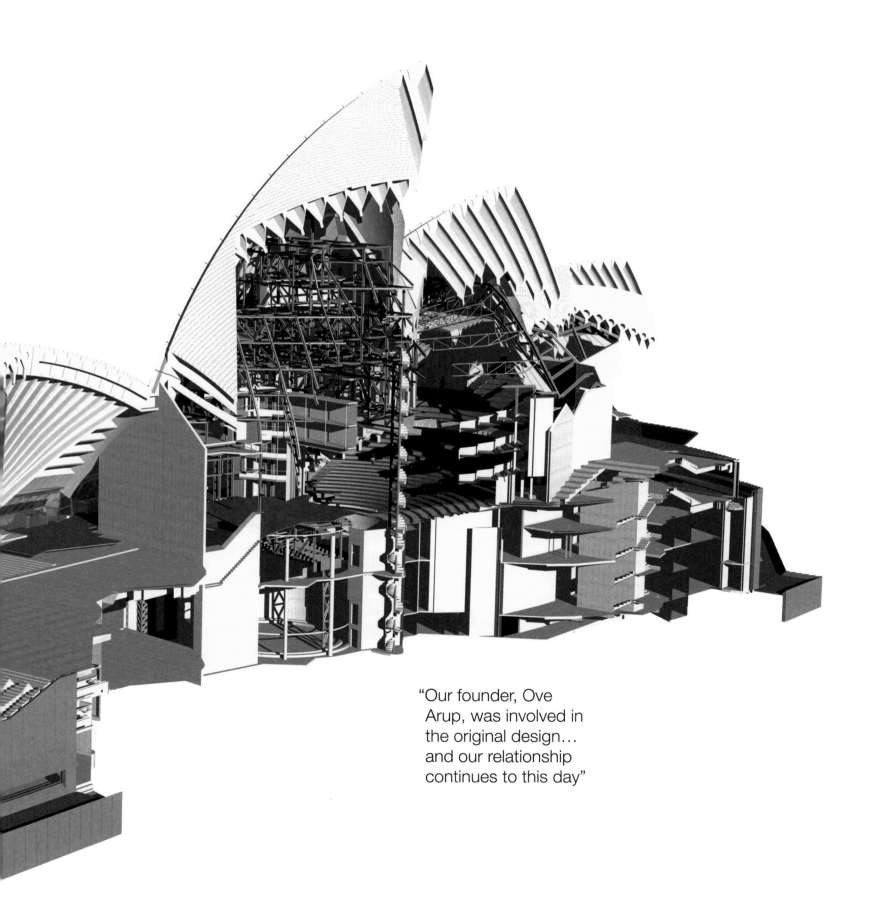

"Our founder, Ove Arup, was involved in the original design… and our relationship continues to this day"

## The show must go on, and on ...

Even icons need a bit of a spruce-up from time to time. And, like other arts venues, the Sydney Opera House had to update its facilities to deal with increasing numbers of visitors.

Our structural digital model for this project was fundamental in a huge overhaul of the traffic system. With 8.2 million visitors each year and 1,000 vehicles arriving and departing each week to keep its six performance spaces and seven restaurants running, this was no simple task.

The original delivery access routes were shared between pedestrians and traffic and they could no longer cope with this combined volume. A new system had to be developed separating pedestrians and traffic for safety and efficiency.

And so the largest building project at the Sydney Opera House since its construction in 1973 began. It included creating a new access tunnel and underground loading dock. This involved tunnelling work underneath the building without disturbing the priceless structure and without interrupting pedestrian access or a show schedule that averages 40 events each week.

To keep the shows on stage, our designers analysed the types of movement that were expected to occur and then assessed their impact on the fabric. We made adjustments to the work in areas where the existing building structure would not tolerate movement.

Since work onsite began in early 2011, construction work has gone on behind the scenes. Meanwhile, all performances and tours have continued as planned, and for the busy shops, cafes and restaurants it's been business as usual.

And the legacy? Visitors can admire Australia's most famous building without worrying about the traffic – and Sydneysiders have an Opera House fit for the 21st century.

**Project name:** Sydney Opera House Venue Improvement Plan (VIP), Vehicle Access and Pedestrian Safety Project (VAPS)
**Designed for:** Sydney Opera House Trust
**Designed with:** VIP – Utzon Architects, Johnson Pilton Walker
VAPS – Utzon Architects, Scott Carver

Can a city
flourish
under a
parasol?

"It was a neighbourhood of dim streets, closed premises, no business and with many empty houses. Now there are no empty premises in the surrounding areas, they are all occupied"

**Dr Leandro Castro**
**Vice President, Cultural Association La Encarnación**

In Seville, the city can flourish both under and over a parasol.

For years Seville's Plaza de la Encarnación was an arid, dead spot acting as a car park between the city's more popular destinations and badly in need of revitalising. Building six vast, interconnected timber 'mushrooms' or 'parasols' that shade the Plaza made it more hospitable to businesses and visitors and transformed a derelict square into one of the city's most exciting landmarks.

The 30m-high parasols were inspired by the vaulted domes of Seville's cathedral and together they form one of the largest timber structures ever built. Using 3D geometry, structural engineers worked to create a network of timber beams to form this enormous frame. We drew on expertise from across the world to come up with a lightweight repetitive connection solution that joined more than 3,000 flat pieces of timber together. The reinforced micro-laminated wood is protected from the elements with a waterproof polyurethane coating.

The result is a magnificent structure – some 150m long, 75m wide and 28m high – which creates a meeting place for local people and business folk and casts shade on the area during the city's hot summers. It works across four intertwined levels, with a viewing platform over an archaeological excavation site at basement level, a farmers' market on the first floor, a square for cultural performances on the second and a restaurant on the third. Most impressive of all is the roof, an undulating walkway with panoramic views over Seville's old quarter.

While the project was being built, the Spanish housing market was collapsing, so the team had to justify public spending. The investment has more than paid off and the parasols have had a major social and commercial impact on the neighbourhood. The once-neglected area is now lively, and empty shops and offices are full. Most important of all, people are now proud to live and work there.

**Project name:** Metropol Parasol, Plaza de la Encarnación
**Designed for:** Gerencia de Urbanismo – Ayuntamiento de Sevilla
**Designed with:** J. Mayer H., Sacyr Vallehermoso

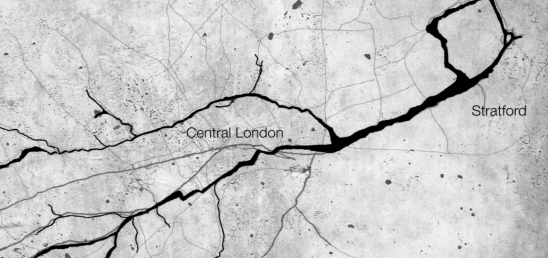

## 1,000+
inspections
were made

## 64
hairline cracks
needed attention

## 120
hours to complete
each repair

## 138,000
cars use the M4 each day

Stratford

Central London

Boston
Manor
flyover

Heathrow
Airport

# Under
# pressure?

Few engineering projects involve plans being drawn up in the morning, rushed to the site and acted on that same afternoon. But that was the reality when a significant crack was found in a key flyover that connects Central London and Heathrow via a motorway artery into the city.

Small cracks had already been discovered in welds that hold together the main parts of the steel girders. We had been asked to find a solution – without closing the road.

But one Friday morning in 2012, engineers discovered a large crack had developed on the Boston Manor viaduct and there was no option but to close the flyover immediately.

The race was on to make sure we could reopen the road in time for key events, including the Olympic and Paralympic Games.

Our teams worked round the clock, supporting a client under pressure from intense media scrutiny and the top levels of government. Our experts in fracture mechanics spent a total of 1,800 hours in just six days, to solve the problem and put traffic back on the road.

**Project name:** Boston Manor Viaduct
**Designed for:** Connect Plus M25
**Designed with:** Highways Agency

# How do you get heat out of a TV studio – and stop sound entering?

An awful lot of heat is inevitably generated by a 24-hour broadcaster, but changing the way ventilation works can remove it without wasting energy.

When BSkyB asked us to design and build an energy-efficient broadcasting centre as part of its aim to become the world's first carbon-neutral broadcaster, we knew we had to think differently. The reason was simple: broadcast centres can produce many times more heat than other buildings but they must be kept cool to keep the equipment and people working well. Traditionally, broadcasters solve this problem by running energy-consuming air-conditioning systems.

Instead, we designed a naturally ventilated space that channels hot air from the studios into a large chimney, integrating an acoustic silencer. At the same time cool air from outside is drawn into the studios from an acoustically lined chamber underneath the building. This system is simple, a bit like lining the studios with very large-scale loft insulation. And the result – a world first – is that they are ventilated while the noise is kept out, essential when recordings are taking place.

Since the building is all about green credentials, other sustainable innovations include shading, rainwater-flushing WCs and a wind turbine to power lighting in the building, which has also become a landmark in West London. There is also a combined cooling, heating and power plant fuelled by waste wood, which helps supply the building's electricity and cooling and recovering waste heat, so there are no boilers.

Sustainability shouldn't get in the way of creativity. The building also had to provide workspace that would give staff creative freedom, so we designed an open and flexible building set round an atrium, also naturally ventilated for much of the year. Staff are encouraged to interact as they meet on the stairs or in the cafés located on every floor.

The result is a multi-award-winning building where staff enjoy their environment and get to produce round-the-clock programming.

The diagram shows a TV studio. Hot air is channelled upwards through a chimney. Cold air is filtered in at the bottom of the building. The sound is kept at bay by the distance the air travels and an acoustic lining

**Project name:** Sky Studios
**Designed for:** BSkyB
**Designed with:** Arup Associates

# How can a university building turn into the teacher?

In the new Engineering Building of the National University of Ireland, Galway, it's not just the professors who do the teaching – it's the building itself. The aim was to build a 'living laboratory' to showcase engineering principles in action. The building also needed to demonstrate its sustainability. It incorporates a biodiverse green roof over the central courtyard, rainwater harvesting for use within the building and a biomass boiler for energy generation.

Occupancy sensors turn off lights and adjust temperatures when people are not in the room; and passive ventilation cools rooms, reducing the need for air conditioning. The building was one of the first in Ireland >

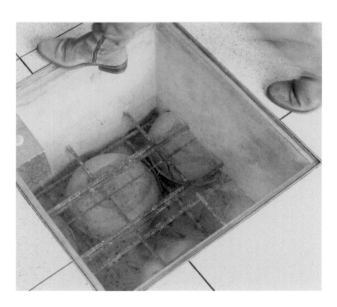

The reinforcement within the concrete walls and the building's foundations is exposed through glass panels

"The design of the building was very helpful for understanding the basic concepts of engineering design. Our lecturers would speak about the building and the way in which it was designed and compare that to the work that we were doing in class. It was great to be able to walk out and see the exposed reinforcement and the exposed pilecaps and understand exactly what we had just learned how to design"

**Maebh Grace, PhD in Civil Engineering**

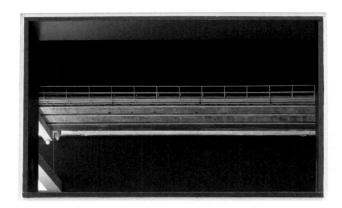

The new Engineering
Building Atrium has
windows onto walkways
and internal spaces

"The building has had a
transforming effect on the
educational environment for
students and the working
environment for staff"

**Padraic O'Donoghue, Professor of Civil Engineering
(below right)**

"Engineering principles are on display the instant you walk through the door of the building into the main atrium. These immediately help to enhance the idea that this is a 'living' building"

**David Byrne, College of Engineering and Informatics**

to use voided slab construction, in which air-filled plastic spheres within the slab reduce the amount of concrete used and $CO_2$ embedded.

The building reflects its function as a place of learning, with parts of its fabric exposed to illustrate engineering principles in action. Students can see the reinforcement in the concrete walls, while the building's foundations are visible under glass panels. Sensors within the building's structure report on the energy demands, strains, temperatures and movements of the building so students can monitor its performance over time.

The building is a centre of engineering excellence in Ireland which has already attracted a record number of applicants and visitors and is set to attract new academic funding. It is proof that every day can be a school day.

**Project name:** Engineering Building, National University of Ireland, Galway
**Designed for:** Buildings and Estates Office, NUI Galway
**Designed with:** RMJM, Taylor Architects

**Can water breathe new life into an old city?**

**Yes, say the people of Bradford**

48

Art with a social function was exactly what Bradford City Council wanted to inject some new life into its old city centre.

We joined the team creating the City Park – a bold, beautiful and flexible space where water has transformed the environment.

The clever design required high-tech water treatment, supply, drainage and storage systems that navigate multiple underground city-centre obstructions such as old foundations and cellars, as well as buried electricity, gas and water services. The centrepiece is a dazzling mirror pool the size of three football pitches.

The multi-functional space is a major feat of civil engineering, design and execution. Its undulating surface ebbs and flows with the rhythms of city life; transforming into a rockpool-peppered causeway where the public can 'walk on water', and again into a full mirror pool that reflects the Grade 1-listed town hall and features a 30m water jet.

But the design goes even further. There is an interactive night-time laser art display. Our work on the acoustics means we are able to mask the sounds of the nearby traffic to create a peaceful idyll at the heart of a busy city.

The people have got their city centre back: once-empty shops are now occupied, the public art installation attracts tourists, and the project pays homage to the Industrial Revolution, when the Bradford Beck river was the lifeblood of the city. In the process we have helped create the UK's largest city-centre water feature and tallest urban fountain, and helped make the people of Bradford proud.

**Project name:** Bradford City Park
**Designed for:** City of Bradford Metropolitan District Council, Gillespies
**Designed with:** The Fountain Workshop, Birse Civils, Sturgeon North Architects

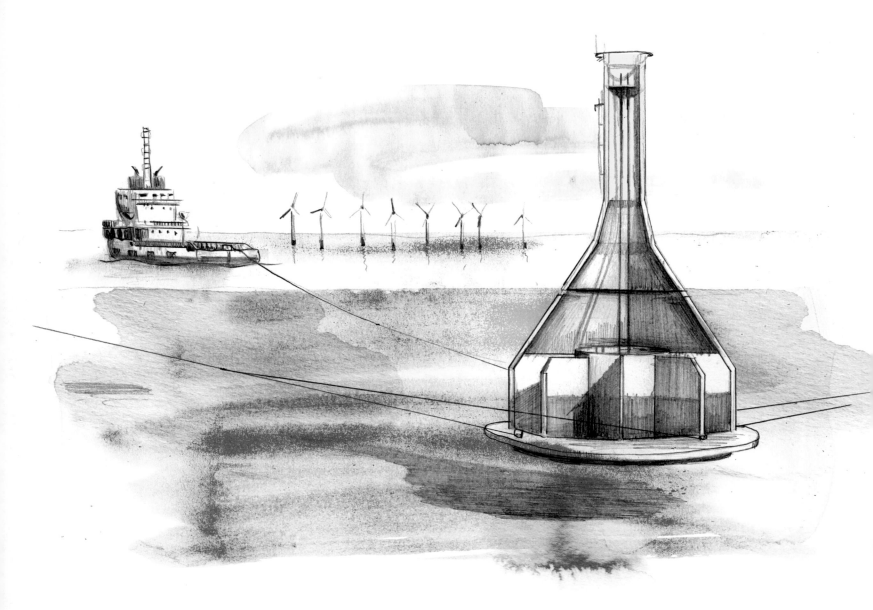

# Can you tow a wind turbine?

Widespread adoption of offshore wind energy has been hampered by the expense of wind-farm construction. Up to now deep-sea wind turbines have required specialist offshore pile installation, which is time consuming, hazardous and harmful to marine life.

Working alongside two partners and pooling our knowledge, we have designed a concrete foundation for deep-sea turbines that can be mass-produced and easily installed. Built on land, the base is a cellular construction, making it buoyant so it can be towed to its location like a boat. Once at its destination, controlled flooding with water means the base can be placed accurately on the sea bed, ready for the turbine to be erected.

This makes wind turbines easier and safer to install than they would be with steel foundations, and makes deep offshore wind farms viable.

And what's the sustainable outcome? Lower turbine installation and maintenance costs spell cheaper renewable energy for the consumers of the future.

**Project name:** GRAVITAS Offshore concrete gravity foundation
**Designed for:** GRAVITAS Offshore Ltd
**Designed with:** Hochtief, Costain

# Are we
# seeing
# TV in a
# whole
# new
# light?

Our report on lighting commissioned by the BBC has brought studio lighting out of the dark ages.

When we were asked by the UK's national broadcaster to assess the latest lighting technologies, including light-emitting diodes (LEDs), we drew on our own technical expertise and the know-how of lighting designers, programme makers and manufacturers from across the industry to measure and analyse different low energy lighting (LEL) solutions. The Carbon Trust, which sponsored the report, approved our findings and these formed the basis of the *Low Energy Lighting Guide for TV Productions*, which is a mine of information for the TV community to use.

A number of BBC programmes have already introduced LEL, with 40% less energy consumed on several productions – showing that the switchover is practical, cost-effective and sustainable.

With an ongoing influence, this is a truly enlightening project.

**Project name:** Low Energy Lighting Guide for TV Productions
**Designed for:** BBC
**Designed with:** BBC

In a congested city,
how do you keep
the traffic flowing?

Infrastructure projects don't come any bigger – or more complex – than the one tackling congestion in Brisbane, one of Australia's fastest-growing cities.

We were asked to design a motorway network linking the city's central business district with its domestic and international airports and northern suburbs. Our scheme comprises a 6.8km road tunnel (Queensland's longest), a 640m flyover and 25 bridges. Much of this technically groundbreaking design involved finding complex tunnelling solutions to minimise disruption to the local community.

The portion of the tunnel excavated by a tunnel boring machine was fitted out with the largest precast steel fibre-reinforced concrete lining in the world. These lining segments were constructed offsite at very efficient rates. To meet the tight 4-year deadline, the tunnelling operations worked 24 hours a day, seven days a week.

Other parts of the tunnel were dug by specialist excavating machines – roadheaders – and at one point 17 of them were operating underground simultaneously.

The finished Airport Link and Northern Busway is transforming traffic flow and reducing an average morning commute of 20 minutes to under five minutes.

All this while keeping the vast majority of the traffic underground and out of sight, ensuring that however the city of Brisbane grows over the next few decades, moving people around freely won't be a problem.

**Project name:** Brisbane Airport Link
**Designed for:** Thiess John Holland joint venture for BrisConnections
**Designed with:** BrisConnections consortium: Macquarie Capital Group Limited, Thiess Pty Ltd, John Holland Pty Ltd, Parsons Brinckerhoff

## The challenge by numbers

# 15km
of tunnels and ramps excavated and lined

# 7km
of entirely new roadway constructed

# 28m
wide, making the Airport Link tunnel the world's largest road cavern

# 125,000
tonnes of reinforcing steel utilised

Cities may be the powerhouses of nations, but collectively they use two-thirds of the world's energy and generate 70% of global $CO_2$ emissions.

However, change is in the air. C40, a network of large and engaged cities from around the world committed to working collaboratively to reduce greenhouse gas emissions and climate risks, commissioned us to analyse and measure the options open to cities in taking positive action to tackle climate change. Chaired by New York City Mayor Michael Bloomberg, C40 currently has 63 cities, which are home to 8% of the global population, produce 12% of global greenhouse gas emissions and account for 21% of global GDP.

Part of C40's mission is to foster the measurement of actions taken to tackle climate change at a local level and then assess mayoral powers to instigate these initiatives.

Through networks focused on common goals and challenges, knowledge is shared among C40 cities so they can have a collective global impact.

The report we co-authored, *Climate Action in Megacities*, aims to guide these cities towards the adoption of more successful strategies to combat climate change. It allows cities to learn from the initiatives others are using – such as encouraging citizens and businesses to cut down on waste and reduce the use of energy in buildings – and thereby evaluate their own climate change efforts.

This was the first report of its kind and included data on 36 megacities, but it's not just a one-off. We'll be completing reports every two years, with the next due to be published in 2014.

**Project name:** Climate Action in Megacities:
C40 Cities Baseline and Opportunities
**Designed for:** C40 Cities: Climate Leadership Group

## The challenge by numbers*

# 4,734

initiatives are currently in effect and another 1,465 are under consideration – we analysed them all

# 300m

tonnes of $CO_2$ per year are emitted by the transport sectors of C40 cities

# 1,343

actions have been implemented by C40 cities to reduce carbon emissions from existing buildings

# 11% to 51%

growth in actions taken to tackle climate issues over four years since C40 inception

*As reported in *Climate Action in Megacities: C40 Cities Baseline and Opportunities* Version 1.0, June 2011

"Buildings are integral to a city's sustainability... When you make buildings more sustainable, this has implications from energy supply to financing"

# A sustainable way of life

Urban regeneration projects are the largest-scale version of recycling that people can practise. They reuse the most constrained asset we have – land. Urban regeneration also encourages all kinds of efficiencies and qualities of life that help build productive societies. For example, an urban regeneration project is already likely to be close to multiple transit lines and connected to stores and residential areas.

Urban regeneration is slowly happening across the world; in Shanghai's Xintiandi area traditional houses have been reformed into a shopping and entertainment district. At C40, we recognise that cities all over the world are already doing dramatic, innovative things on climate change and overall sustainability. So our task is less about advocacy and more about helping cities do their existing jobs better, faster and more thoughtfully.

Cities are leading the charge against climate change. First, they are more efficient. The physical landscape of a city means there are shorter distances, more opportunities for mass transit and smaller living spaces in general.

Second, the solutions to fight climate change – such as using mass transit or making buildings more energy efficient – come more naturally to urban populations. Buildings are integral to a city's sustainability. In New York, they account for 75% of the city's carbon emissions. So any strategy aimed at making New York more carbon efficient has buildings at its heart – the most important engineering in the city takes place on reconstruction and renovation projects.

The opposite is true in cities in emerging markets and developing economies, where the emphasis is more on the construction of new projects.

Of course, nothing is simple in a large city. When you make existing buildings more sustainable, this has implications from energy supply to financing. Thinking through these implications and coming up with solutions to help ease the process of sustainability is central to so many of today's design projects.

**Dr. Rohit Aggarwala**, Special Advisor to C40 Chair, Mayor of New York City Michael R. Bloomberg, and former Director of Long-Term Planning and Sustainability for New York City

# What's the best way to lay tracks for America's next great railway?

Planning a railway to whisk passengers, at high speed, through the state of California is challenging, not least because of the hundreds of miles of disparate terrain it will cross. From floodplains and wetlands to mountains and deserts, the track will serve a population that lives in a mix of dense urban environments, small communities and remote rural farms.

Our experience was called upon to find the most efficient route, but one that also minimised impact on the environment and was economically beneficial to the towns it was to run through. Elevated viaducts needed to be less than 100m tall and tunnels needed to be kept as short as possible to minimise cost. The route crosses several geological faults, but tunnels and viaducts needed to avoid crossing faults wherever possible. We also needed to limit horizontal curves and vertical gradients to maximise speed. This meant considering thousands of potential options.

To meet the challenge we used geographic information system software to log all geotechnical, seismic, hydraulic, hydrology, drainage and flood control data about the region and then analyse it according to different criteria, to devise the best route options. The system helped the team review and rule out hundreds of possibilities quickly before choosing the best option.

**Project name:** California High-Speed Rail Plan
**Designed for:** California High-Speed Rail Authority
**Designed with:** Hatch Mott MacDonald, URS Corporation

# CAN BUSIER MEAN BETTER?

It might sound like a contradiction, but by expanding one of the world's busiest airports, we are proportionally reducing its ecological impact. One condition of expansion, set out by the Airport Authority Hong Kong, was that the green agenda be firmly in mind when planning to increase capacity by adding a Midfield Concourse. This sits between the two main runways at Hong Kong International Airport (HKIA).

Passengers will wait for flights in cool comfort behind solar heat-reflecting glazing in the floor-to-ceiling windows, which will minimise heat and the need for air conditioning. Meanwhile, recycled water will cool the chillers that provide necessary air conditioning, and low-voltage lighting with daylight sensors will be complemented by skylights that maximise natural light. Behind the scenes, waste and water will be recycled, seawater will be used for flushing toilets and solar panels on the roof will reduce energy consumption.

As well as saving operating costs, these initiatives are expected to achieve energy savings of more than 20%, making HKIA one of the world's greenest airports.

The Midfield Concourse, which is due to be completed in 2015, aims to be the world's first airport building to be awarded a BEAM Plus Gold rating for sustainability – one of the highest ratings for a building's environmental performance recognised by the Hong Kong Building Council.

**Project name:** HKIA Midfield Development
**Designed for:** Airport Authority Hong Kong
**Designed with:** Mott MacDonald, Aedas, Atkins

# What would tempt you out of your car?

There is no easy way to encourage people to get out of their cars and instead travel by bike, foot or public transport. But the Phoenix, Arizona region's Maricopa Association of Governments (MAG) is trying to do just that, by better integrating land use and transportation.

Our analysis brought together urban design, economic analysis, spatial planning and travel demand. We were able to then map it against the region's plans for transport investment. We also added in the human dimension, engaging local stakeholders to better understand the region's needs.

Armed with this knowledge, we delivered a set of tools to MAG. These allow smarter investment and policy decisions to guide future development and link the region with high-capacity public transport service. And ultimately, people in Maricopa County may get to live in a region with a sustainable transportation system.

**Project name:** Sustainable Transportation and Land Use Integration Study
**Designed for:** Maricopa Association of Governments

# Can technology breathe new life into a neighbourhood?

The business district of Oakland, Pittsburgh, was a successful neighbourhood with lots of potential, but its austere, brutalist 1950s and 1960s architecture and confusing streetscape made it an uninviting place.

Oakland Business Improvement District asked us to find ways to make the area more aesthetically pleasing, inspiring and easy to navigate, which would attract visitors and stimulate enthusiasm for the creative and technological businesses in the area.

Our answer was to marry technical and design expertise to improve the district in three ways: functionally, through improved signage and wayfinding; place-making, through art, including sculpture, landscaping and multimedia walls; and, experientially, via technology, soundscapes and light.

Now the neighbourhood is much more accessible and appealing. Oakland's streetscape is peppered with innovations designed to delight and inform visitors. The area is dotted with intelligent street lamps that have the capability to emit WiFi and display information, such as local news and weather forecasts, to passers-by.

And we've helped bring Oakland right up to date.

**Project name:** Innovation Oakland
**Designed for:** Oakland Business Improvement District
**Designed with:** !melk, EDGE Studio, Billings Jackson

# Nancy Kete

## Designing with resilience in mind

# "Resilience thinking is the best way to look at problems in a world that becomes more complex every day"

Resilience is a vital concept in developmental space and environmental thinking. It is what enables people, the communities they live in and the systems they depend on to survive, adapt and thrive no matter what is thrown at them.

The Rockefeller Foundation celebrates its centenary in 2013 and our mission remains unchanged: to enhance the condition of humanity. Right now, we do that by sharpening our goals around building resilience to chronic stresses and sudden shocks, and promoting equitable growth.

Humanity and the planet we live on face many hazards and sources of vulnerability. Resilience helps us overcome these vulnerabilities and anticipate, withstand and recover from the hazards. This is not something you achieve once and then move on – it is a state of mind that is realistic about the threats facing the world.

Resilience thinking is the best way to look at problems in a world that becomes more complex every day. Given how quickly problems are accelerating, only resilience thinking will help us reduce our vulnerabilities.

Responsibility for building this resilience lies with everybody. We know that making a city resilient, for example, depends on work that is mostly done at a neighbourhood level. But that neighbourhood work can only do so much and is ultimately dependent on the abilities of elected officials, or the companies you have been paying to provide services and infrastructure.

Resilience is a nested concept within any given city. Building a new resilient transportation system depends on the resilience of the infrastructure that the system relies on. It is almost impossible to make something resilient in isolation. You can make one thing the focus, but you always have to look a level up or a level down to ensure that the project is truly resilient.

It is clear that the world of the near future is not going to be like the world of the past, even for no other reason than climate change. The best designers are recognising this and working with their clients to make sure that they design with resilience at the front of their minds. They must design so buildings will perform well in the future, knowing that there is some uncertainty about how exactly the future is going to be.

This is not just about defence against changes in the future. New installations must also avoid contributing to worsening situations with regards to energy efficiency, water use and passive survivability. The buildings of the future should not only be efficient in normal operating situations, but as survivable and comfortable as possible when there are disruptions to infrastructure. This is all part of the design and engineering challenges in a resilient world.

**Nancy Kete** is Managing Director of the Rockefeller Foundation

The Rockefeller Foundation supports work that expands opportunity and strengthens resilience to social, economic, health and environmental challenges

# How can a wheelchair user exit a burning building?

Great – and effective – design is often about turning received wisdom on its head. One such assumption is that elevators are a no-go during a blaze in a building.

In China, which is home to 33% of the world's buildings taller than 200m, this is a particularly concerning issue. Even very fit people would find it hard to escape from the top floors in an emergency. For those less physically able, the challenge is even greater.

So when we were asked to design evacuation strategies for high-rise projects in China, we came up with a radical solution. Our suggestion was to use elevators to supplement staircases as exit routes. Our team designed elevator shafts robust enough to resist fire and smoke, which work alongside already mandatory refuge floors where people can wait safely. Our elevator evacuation has been approved by the Chinese authorities for implementation in the design of the Shanghai World Financial Center, the Ping An International Finance Center and Kingkey 100 buildings in Shenzhen, and for a new mass transit railway line in Hong Kong. Our innovation will contribute to the improvement of fire safety standards and protect the lives of thousands in China – and potentially more worldwide.

**Project name:** Shanghai WFC, Ping An IFC, Kingkey 100 Finance Tower
**Designed for:** Mori Building Co. Ltd., Ping An Insurance (Group), Kingkey Group
**Designed with:** Kohn Pedesen Fox Associates (KPF), (Shanghai WFC and Ping An IFC)

# Gender and the city: does it make a difference in urban planning?

Cities shouldn't just evolve by chance. Socio-cultural factors have an important role to play, so we need to understand these factors to help plan urban areas. Women, for instance, are more likely to plan their travel routes around cities based on their personal safety. They will choose to walk if routes are safe, but they are also more likely than men to use public transport.

When we are trying to achieve something in particular – such as designing a low carbon city or encouraging people to opt for greener modes of transport – understanding such nuances helps us make informed decisions. Fine-tuning the environment can improve the take-up of public transport.

To understand these issues better, we work with sociologists and anthropologists. We recently funded research into how psychological and socio-cultural factors influence people's behaviour in the urban context.

It revealed that age, ethnicity and socio-economic level, as well as gender, need to influence the way cities are designed. With these issues in mind, urban developers can create towns and cities that are more appropriate for the people that actually live there.

**Project name:** The Cities and People Project
**Designed with:** Institute for Environmental Entrepreneurship

How big does a
dog playground
need to be?

Wall Street is synonymous with Gordon Gekko and financial giants. But today there is a new attraction. The East River, at the foot of New York's financial district, has been transformed from a derelict wasteland into a vibrant waterfront park.

Even dogs have their own playground – 4,750 square feet, complete with a climbing bridge, sandpit, splash pad and dog-house.

Bringing to life a 2-mile stretch that is partly tucked under FDR Drive is part of Mayor Bloomberg's vision to revitalise Manhattan's waterfront. Using our design know-how, Pier 15 was transformed into a >

"I love the new waterfront. It's a pleasure to walk around the rivers in Manhattan now. It was pretty horrible before"
**Inez Kirby**

new 2-level structure, with a café and educational centre below, and lawns and seating areas at both levels, offering sensational views of New York Harbor. At night the area changes as the pale purple girder under the highway is lit.

As the site is subject to flooding, special dispensation was obtained to apply a process called 'wet floodproofing' to accommodate water entering the building in the event of flooding, because height constraints made >

"The esplanade is great. It's actually more relaxed than the West Side. I love the chairs. It felt like walking into a rooftop party"
Emmanuel Guervil

"We've been coming to this area for more than ten years. It's much nicer now and more friendly for families. We're happy for that"

**Marixsa Rodriguez**

it impossible to raise the building to comply with the New York City Building Code requirements. We also advised on materials to weather the marine environment.

The vision for East River Waterfront Esplanade includes adapting existing Pier 35, which will have a 35m-high green wall and a tidal slot cut into it, creating a home for various types of marine life.

Already this previously neglected corner of Manhattan is a magnet for joggers, sunbathers, pedestrians and cyclists – and dogs – and is generating new interest in a forgotten part of New York.

**Project name:** East River Waterfront Esplanade
**Designed for:** New York City Economic Development Corporation
**Designed with:** SHoP Architects, Daniel Frankfurt, Ken Smith

# Can you make a park underground?

It might sound extraordinary, but New Yorkers have seen glimpses of how an old underground tram station could be transformed into a park.

Capturing daylight is a critical element to the success of this project, which will give a new lease of life to the dark, early 20th-century tram station.

Our team, bringing together geotechnical engineers, lighting designers and fire/life safety consultants, analysed the space in the heart of the Lower East Side and revealed how it could become a well-lit, inviting underground park.

The existing space, disused since 1948, has no sunlight because of its position below a wide and busy road.

Sun-tracking mirrors were proposed to redirect light through highly reflective pipes. This would, in turn, illuminate the indoor space, allowing plants to grow.

The underground site could give the local community a park as well as a flexible space for performance, a soft-landscaped area with plants and even somewhere to eat.

Channelling sunlight into the subterranean space might sound like chasing a rainbow – but in New York the sun really might shine underground.

**Project:** The Lowline
**Designed for:** Underground Development Foundation
**Designed with:** RAAD Studio, HR&A Advisors,
Ed Jacobs, Lorne Whitehead

# If an orchestra wants the best sound, is it just about finely tuned instruments?

It's about to be showtime all the time at Virginia Tech University's new Center for the Arts. When it opens fully to the public in late 2013, it will be as comfortable putting on Bach as hosting a Broadway-style musical.

In smaller communities, where there isn't demand for multiple venues, a single arts centre needs to serve many needs. This requires more than rearranging a set or hanging a different backdrop. For an audience to get the best possible experience of a show, these multi-purpose halls need to be able to change their room acoustic to suit particular styles of performance.

As acousticians we set out to combine sound excellence with flexible, cutting-edge technical systems at Virginia Tech. We developed 3D accoustic models in our SoundLab to test every element in the main performance hall – from the stage layout to the reflector and balcony shaping. This meant the building owners, design team members and our acousticians could actually listen to how different types of performance would sound before the room was built.

We worked with the architects to ensure that the acoustics in the centre, which includes a 1,260-seat hall, galleries and a research area, will deliver optimum sound quality for every type of performer, whether they are a solo singer or part of a swing band. Motorised acoustic drapes will absorb sound and reduce reverberation, and the large orchestra shell reflects the sound back towards the audience. This shell can enhance the music played by a band or orchestra and be instantly retracted for a ballet performance or play.

Users will be able to adapt the space's acoustics with the flick of a control-panel switch, transforming it from concert hall to theatre in just a few minutes. That's how to put on a show.

**Project name:** Center for the Arts at Virginia Tech
**Designed for:** Virginia Polytechnic Institute and State University
**Designed with:** Snohetta, STV Architects

**Move to the beat:** colour pigments dancing on a speaker show that by capturing vibrations sound waves are made visible

## How would you like your cultural centre?

When the people of the Japanese city of Yurihonjo were invited to contribute ideas for their cultural centre, working on the result was never going to be straightforward.

"There was a keen desire to include local residents in planning the use of the building," says Mr Muraoka, Chairman of Kadare Voluntary Committee. "The Voluntary Committee consists of around 50 citizen volunteers ranging in age from their 20s to their 70s."

Ongoing conversations between the architect and the local community led to the creation of a space that gives the community everything it asked for, including a complex, striking design.

The multi-purpose 3-floor building includes retail and cultural spaces, a 1,100-seat theatre, a library, a music studio, a storytelling room and a traditional Japanese tearoom. Most striking of all is the planetarium, which appears to float above the library, supported only by four diagonal columns.

Of course, delivering a building that was to be all things to all people presented its own set of challenges.

Reach for the stars: the planetarium at Yurihonjo's cultural centre was designed in collaboration with the people of the city

As the structural engineer, we had to be prepared to make major changes, often quickly. We had to respond to sometimes tricky feedback that included comments such as "a straight passage is dull". We were able to make changes rapidly by using Rhinoceros 3D software to translate the architect's physical designs into detailed digital models, allowing us to amend and analyse the structure.

And we made residents' dreams a reality. The end result includes a winding 'gathering street', peppered with skylights, which connects all areas of the centre, as well as a theatre that can be transformed into ten different configurations through mobile seating.

It's an unusual, magical space that not only inspires Yurihonjo's people, but has also captured the imaginations of 570,000 visitors so far – four times more than expected. Who says dreams can't come true?

**Project name:** Kadare Cultural Centre
**Designed for:** Yurihonjo City
**Designed with:** Chiaki Arai Urban and Architecture Design

How

did

this

fig

tree

inspire

a

building's

design?

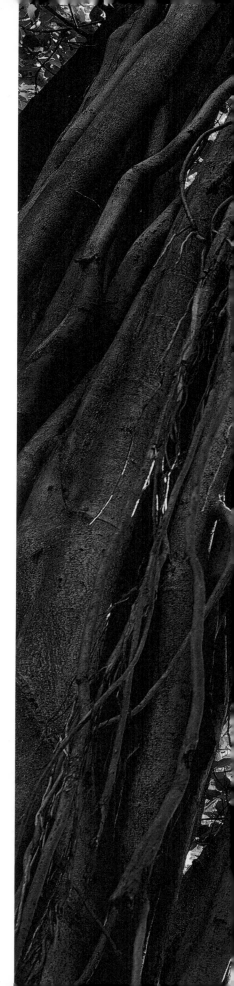

Few buildings take their inspiration from nature in quite the same way as Brisbane's tallest office block.

One One One Eagle Street's design is based on the way plants grow towards the light – and the idea originated very close to home. Across the street are the Moreton Bay fig trees, which inspired key parts of the structure.

The distinctive fig-tree columns aren't just there to look cool – they hold up the building. Our design engineers wanted to create maximum floor space, light and views for the building users. But the 50-storey tower's narrow plot was constrained on either side by two existing towers, above a car park and on difficult ground next to the river. And construction had to be carried out without disturbing activity in the congested surrounding retail and office precinct, and the basement of the site itself.

This complexity brought a significant design challenge: the building's core could only be in the south-west of the plot, and because it was off-centre it could not withstand wind loads. To counter this we created cross-columns, which were not only inspired by the way fig trees grow, giving the building a unique appearance, but also gave the building stability in the wind. By transferring loads we were also able to build a high, open lobby, supported >

"Due to the architecture, design and engineering there were a lot of qualities that were key selling points for tenants, such as the interesting spaces created by the configuration of slender columns. These really set the building apart from anything else on the market. There is no doubt that One One One Eagle Street is one of Australia's leading buildings"

**Jamie Nelson, Project Director, The GPT Group**

by as few columns as possible. This is a public plaza through which pedestrians can move between the river, adjacent offices and retail areas, and local public transport services.

To reach this sophisticated engineering solution, we created a computer formula to generate a number of configurations that the columns could take, based on the way plants grow towards the light. Some 2 million random column sets were created and the most structurally efficient were identified. We selected the ones that best complemented the design. The columns taper towards the roof, measuring from just 800mm at ground level to a slender 300mm at the top.

Engineering students came to watch as we used an innovative top-down construction technique that involved supporting the basement excavation with steel plunge columns so we could dig down and build up at the same time. It cut the build process by about a year and saved millions of dollars.

One One One Eagle Street is proof that taking inspiration from nature really can help grow a building.

**Project name:** One One One Eagle Street
**Designed for:** The GPT Group
**Designed with:** Cox Rayner Architects

UPDATING THE BRIDGE WILL HELP TO CREATE AROUND 3,000 LOCAL JOBS A YEAR

15% OF IMPORTED GOODS IN THE US ARE TRUCKED ACRO

# How do you update a bridge?

In Southern California, the 1960s bridge that brings 15% of the US's imported goods from Long Beach to Terminal Island is no longer fit for purpose.

The old bridge does not have sufficient clearance to accommodate the next generation of cargo ships and it has also become more expensive to maintain while struggling to handle increasing traffic volumes. So the Port of Long Beach sought the most cost-effective replacement possible.

We drew on the expertise of our worldwide teams across disciplines from bridge design and highway operations to seismic and lighting, to develop a proposal that offered the best value not only in terms of construction and maintenance, but also in terms of speed of completion.

Our design for this project, with an overall cost of nearly US$1bn, included a cable-stayed bridge with two attractive and structurally efficient tapered towers. This is geared to help protect users in the event of an earthquake and allow a more efficient flow of traffic onto the bridge.

The construction work is supporting an essential artery for the US economy, creating an expected 3,000 jobs locally each year.

It's not a project that will be completed overnight. But the 5-year construction process is underway to create a 6-lane bridge – the two additional lanes will safely carry the increasing number of trucks and commuter cars that rely on it – with enough clearance for the next generation of cargo ships. And the bridge will be brought right up to date.

**Project name:** Gerald Desmond Bridge Replacement Project
**Designed for:** Caltrans, The Port of Long Beach, SFI joint venture
**Designed with:** Biggs Cardosa Associates

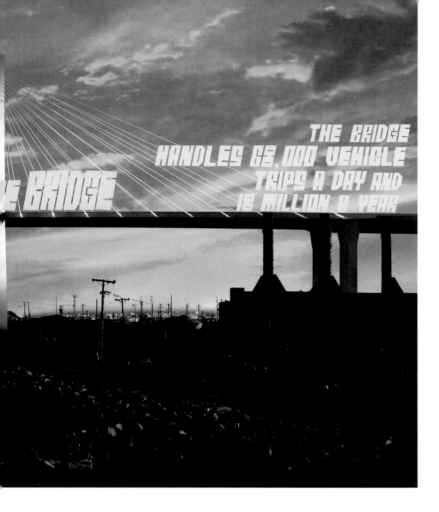

THE BRIDGE
HANDLES 65,000 VEHICLE
TRIPS A DAY AND
15 MILLION A YEAR

# Can you revitalise a run-down waterfront?

Imagine the scene: people strolling from the historic centre of Santos in the Brazilian state of São Paulo on to a new esplanade packed with buzzing shops, restaurants, hotels, university buildings, cultural centres, offices and even a museum dedicated to local football hero Pelé.

We were asked to plan the best way to transform the land that runs along the port into a lively hub. Bringing this vision to life will be a challenge. It is a restricted sliver of land, divided from the city centre by a busy road, a railway track and a row of run-down historic warehouses that can't be moved; and limited by the traffic necessary to service the world's largest-capacity cruise terminal and South America's largest port.

With skills in urban and waterfront design, and including transport planning and economic feasibility analysis in the study, we have shown it is possible to revitalise without radically altering the existing environment.

Our urban study has created a framework for development that is now being used to attract bids from private investors to support public funding and so realise our plans.

A Pelé museum might still be a dream; but we have shown it could become a reality.

**Project name:** Santos Valongo waterfront regeneration
**Designed for:** World Bank, City of Santos

# Girish Menon

## Clean water is the key to progress in the developing world

Water and sanitation is the fundamental first step to getting people out of poverty. It improves people's lives, restores human dignity where it is lacking, and is vital for eliminating infectious diseases such as diarrhoea, cholera and typhoid.

Sanitation is vital to better health, better education, gender equality and dignity. In poor parts of south Asia and sub-Saharan Africa, for example, you will see more teenage girls in school in areas that have access to safe water.

But its impact reaches even further. The World Bank's Water and Sanitation Programme has studied the economic cost of a lack of clean water and sanitation on the developing world's economies. It has estimated that the economic cost to countries in south Asia and Africa of not having safe water is anywhere between 2% and 7% of GDP. So, there is a huge economic gain to be made from finding ways to improve access to safe water in the developing world.

Working with national and regional governments, local organisations and designers and engineers, who are passionate about improving people's lives and overcoming technical barriers in the local context, is essential to the success of projects.

Such partnerships can ensure that safe drinking water is available, and to help people in communities where it isn't, by developing skills at a local level. Providing access to clean water can have a dramatic impact on the economic conditions of individuals and communities.

The Kombogara Village in the mountains of Papua New Guinea is one example. To source the 20 litres each person needs every day, women and children had to make up to three trips up and down the rugged hills daily to collect water – often barefoot and sometimes in darkness.

In hilly areas, like this, we have worked with specialists to design gravity-fed schemes that allow water to be piped down to communities from higher water sources. The spring or small unpolluted stream is tapped, dammed and protected at its source before being piped down to storage tanks in villages. Distribution pipes then feed protected tap stands allowing people to draw water close to their homes. The community is trained to maintain the system independently.

As a result of this project, co-funded by Arup and the European Commission's Rural Water Supply and Sanitation Project, the community now has access to spring water from several tap points in the village. A task that took at least an hour now takes five minutes and women in the community save approximately 91,000 hours a year.

One villager commented: "The new water taps help me a lot. They will give me time to look after my younger children and I have more time to spend at the market, earning money for their education."

By combining design know-how with local knowledge, we not only produce the best solutions, but create systems that have a much broader positive impact on the lives of those who need them.

As a social enterprise, Arup has been a strong supporter of WaterAid since choosing the organisation as its charitable partner in 2006 to mark Arup's 60th birthday. Staff worldwide enthusiastically raise money or donate their time and expertise to projects in much of the developing world.

**Girish Menon** is Director, International Programmes at WaterAid

"By combining design know-how with local knowledge we create solutions that have a much broader impact on the lives of those who need them"

# Can a megacity get clean water to a million people...

Supplying clean water to a booming capital such as Manila in the Philippines remains a problem in the 21st century. With a rapidly growing population and being located in a seismically active region, the capital needs a water supply that is safe, secure and resilient.

The East La Mesa Water Treatment Plant at the La Mesa Dam goes a long way to addressing this problem and will transform the lives of a million Manila residents.

While managing the tendering process for this, Manila Water's first major water treatment plant, we improved on plans for the location and delivery of safe, clean and cheap water, saving money and improving overall energy efficiency in the process.

The plant will boost the local economy by delivering a cheaper and more reliable supply of clean water to homes and businesses, while also providing the opportunity to recharge depleting groundwater reservoirs.

**Project name:** East La Mesa Water Treatment Plant
**Designed for:** MANILA WATER

Cleaning up Manila: ensuring the water of life flows to millions of people

# ... and keep
# it flowing to
# millions more?

Our work in Manila is not just about creating new water facilities. It is also about reusing old structures, which can be more sustainable than creating new ones, saving on money and materials.

Manila Water asked us to rehabilitate two decommissioned pipelines located inside the capital, which already has 12 million residents and is still growing. We repaired the pipelines, applying a system not previously used in the Philippines – a fibre-reinforced polymer structural interior lining for the cast iron pipe.

By extending the life of the pipelines for another 50 years we provided an inexpensive, low-maintenance solution with low environmental impact.

In a developing city without widespread access to clean water, a marriage of efficiency and sustainability is a perfect match.

**Project name:** AQ2 and A Rita Water Pipeline
**Designed for:** MANILA WATER

How
do you

## food in the heart of a city?

There aren't many cities where the food is so local it was sourced only a block away.

As more people move to China's urban centres to take advantage of city amenities, valuable farming and growing skills are being lost, leading to a reliance on imported food. The Beijing Eco Valley aims to address this problem, balancing inhabitants' needs for modern metropolitan services with a sustainable, low carbon, quality domestic food supply. It seeks to develop agrarian skills, rather than lose them.

Work has started on the 10-year construction of a community in China's Fangshan District, 40km from Beijing. Among the city's 60,000 new residents, a relocated existing population of farmers will be trained in our 'beyond organic' approach, which takes the principles of organic farming to the next level by focusing primarily on healthy soil biology combined with new techniques. The aim is to reduce

chemical use, focus on nutrient quality and adopt global best practices for food safety.

We developed a novel approach to masterplanning that integrates residential, commercial and industrial zoning with tracts of land for agricultural demonstration, research and food production.

While the community will have farmland and greenhouses at its heart, its people will also enjoy access to schools, hospitals, research facilities, hotels, shopping and other city amenities and employment opportunities within walking and biking distance.

It may be the first time that the concept of 'farm-to-table' has generated not a restaurant, but a whole new city.

**Project name:** COFCO Agricultural Eco Valley
**Designed for:** COFCO Corporation
**Designed with:** Moore Ruble Yudell Architects & Planners, Pure Design LLC

Can a
brick
change
a life?

When our team of engineers travelled to north-east Uganda to help build a vocational school and clinic for young people, they developed the building blocks for a sustainable future – literally and metaphorically.

Our volunteers at the school in the Teso region needed a construction method that was achievable with the resources available. Their solution was a system of Interlocking Stabilised Soil Blocks (ISSBs), something we had used in a previous project. Unlike traditional blocks, ISSBs don't need to be fired, making them quicker to construct. And, because they interlock rather than using mortar, the financial and environmental costs are lowered. A further benefit came because the community was able to use local materials to build instead of concrete and steel.

The sustainable benefits of the school go further. Its curvaceous leaf-shaped design means huge amounts of rainwater can be collected during the wet season and harvested for the dry season, sustaining a whole village. And the introduction of internal ventilated composting toilets, new to the region, is improving sanitation for the villagers and staving off disease.

The legacy lives on: by transferring our technical knowledge and showing people how to build using locally sourced materials, we gave the community the tools to build schools and a better life for the people in the region.

**Project name:** Shalom International School
**Designed for:** Teso Educational Support Services (TESS), Teso Region

# Can a building make you feel better?

## When you ask the patients what they want, it can

"The clever thing about the hospital is that it has design and functionality. It's not dull or white or clinical – it's colourful and uplifting. It's probably very easy for people to say it's just a building, but it's not. It's clearly been considered with patients in mind"

**Ben Russell, 51, patient,
being treated for bowel and liver cancer**

"When I first saw the building I didn't believe it was a hospital; it's so beautiful and a great place to work. I really think the environment makes people feel better. For me, the best part of the building is the roof garden. I go there on my break – it's very unusual to have a space like that"

**Kingsley Okorie, Macmillan Cancer Centre Concierge**

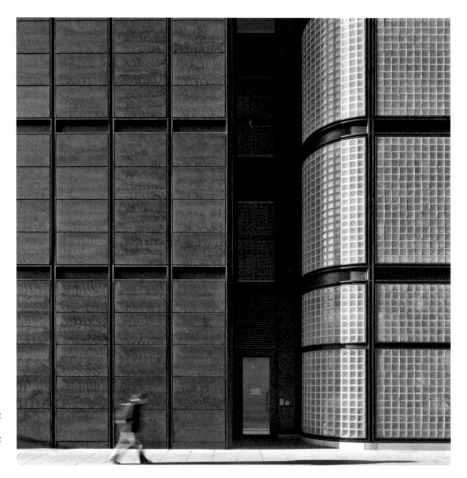

From the outside it does not look like a typical hospital. Glass is a theme throughout the building, which is flooded with natural light

The first of its kind outside the United States, the new University College London Hospital (UCLH) Macmillan Cancer Centre is a revolution in cancer care. As treatments for cancer advance and patients require fewer and shorter stays in hospital, our challenge was to take as a starting point the needs of patients and their carers and design a building that was welcoming to outpatients and complementary to the new style of treatment the hospital provides.

Patients and carers were involved throughout the design – helping to choose the building's beautiful, bright furnishings and fittings. The building is a comfortable and pleasant place to visit and offers a sanctuary where patients can live with the realities of their condition.     >

Left: a view from underneath
the rooftop 'healing garden'.
Right: The rooftop 'healing
garden' is a space where
patients and carers can enjoy
quiet relaxation

The 7-storey walk-in, walk-out cancer centre offers
fully integrated cancer treatment, with floors dedicated
to the different aspects of cancer treatment, as well as
facilities for clinical research, including the UK's first
PET MRI scanner.

To bring a bright, spacious feel, the double-height floors
allow natural light to flood the building. We employed an
innovative glazing system that has not only met National
Health Service environmental targets eight years early,
but also cuts carbon emissions by a third. Glass is a
theme throughout the building, in particular on the
rooftop 'healing garden'. This space offers an open-air
sanctuary for patients and carers, while the plant room's
roof is home to the photovoltaic panels that provide
onsite energy generation. Elsewhere, the use of exposed
concrete not only looks architecturally beautiful and adds
a feeling of warmth, but it recovers heat, helping keep >

"The room where I do wig fittings has lots of natural light flooding into it, which is really important if you want to appreciate the colours of the wigs or scarves. One of my patients calls it an 'oasis' and I think that's an apt word"

**Nicola Panara, Support Information Assistant and wig fitter, Macmillian Information Centre**

"Patients would never normally have the opportunity to meet each other but here they wait in cleverly designed 'pod-style' waiting areas. Knowing that they're all here to be treated for a urology condition gives them the confidence to start conversations and support each other"

**Hazel McBain, Senior Research Nurse, Urology**

Left: Urology treatment area.
Right: Open-plan social
area on the chemotherapy
treatment floor

conditions stable throughout the year. This clever design
is also environmentally efficient.

Our team of acousticians ensured there is total privacy
from room to room, while our lighting specialists looked
at the best solutions to reduce glare while providing
lighting levels staff need. Our fire strategy has reduced
the number of fire compartments and halved the number
of stairs, which has allowed for the modern, open-plan
treatment bays and kept the flow of the building.

The result? A modern approach to cancer care that puts
patients at the heart of the design.

**Project name:** UCH Macmillan Cancer Centre
**Designed for:** University College London Hospitals
NHS Foundation Trust (UCLH)
**Designed with:** Hopkins Architects, Skanska

## When does
## rain start play?

At the Australian Open Tennis Championship rainwater was, surprisingly, key to ensuring the tournament remained in its Melbourne home. A decade-long drought in Victoria made rainwater harvesting a major focus for the redevelopment of Melbourne Park's ageing facilities.

The prospect of losing the Open emerged when the contract between the Victorian Government and Tennis Australia approached expiry and Sydney's Government began to show an interest in hosting the event.

But the additional environmental and sustainability factors of a water-harvesting project as part of the redevelopment of the park demonstrated the Victorian Government's ability to maintain the grounds in the future.

After our team carried out a water-management study, looking at rainfall reliability and testing water quality,

we proposed a system to capture stormwater. The 4.5ML underground concrete tank and filtration treatment will also produce high-quality recycled water to keep the grounds and surrounds clean and green.

It is the first scheme of its kind at a major grand slam venue. With the vision realised, the system now supplies about 45ML of treated stormwater each year at Melbourne Park for use in irrigation, toilet flushing and cleaning – a 70% reduction in drinking water use at the venue.

That's game, set, and match to Melbourne Park.

**Project name:** MOPT Stormwater Harvesting Scheme
**Designed for:** Victorian Government and Melbourne and Olympic Parks Trust

Catching rainfall; Rod Laver Arena, the Australian Open Grand Slam tennis tournament, January 2013

How do villagers safely get from here...

# ... to here?

In a remote part of Yunnan Province in China, 3,000 people from six different villages rely on a single bridge to connect them with schools, supplies and farmland. But the original weak bamboo structure was regularly destroyed by floods, forcing people to find a different crossing over the fast-flowing river, sometimes adding up to seven hours to their round trip.

A new bridge was the only option. We offered technical support to Wu Zhi Qiao, a charitable foundation, to help build the 20m bridge. The project was a combination of design skill, goodwill and luck. We asked our global network of staff for a design solution and, after receiving 44 designs, more than 1,200 staff, friends, family, charity connections and student networks voted for their favourite. Steel factory S-couvrot sponsored the project, allowing us to design and construct the bridge for just £25,000.

But even with all this support in place, most of the hard work was still to come. We had to identify a flood-safe spot and motivate a team of 49 skilled and unskilled volunteers to construct the bridge onsite. Getting machinery to the remote location was impossible, so we hand-built a suspension cable using locally sourced bamboo, steel wires and anchor pulleys. It meant we could put the galvanised steel for the bridge in place.

Thanks to our engineering spirit and design passion, local people can now cross the river, and they have the skills to maintain the bridge into the future.

**Project name:** Wu Zhi Qiao Bridge
**Designed for:** Wu Zhi Qiao Charitable Foundation, Mixia Village
**Designed with:** S-couvrot, students from Kunming University of Science and Technology, Chinese University of Hong Kong, Hong Kong University of Science and Technology

## The challenge by numbers

### 500km
from Kunming, the nearest major city – the journey takes 11 hours by car through hilly terrain

### 1.5km
between the bridge and the nearest village. It can only be accessed by foot – all equipment had to be carried to the site and it could only be worked on in daylight

### 22
of our volunteers lived in the village, sleeping in villagers' houses

### 12
days to carry out the work, during the Christmas holidays

# Can a town ever keep its feet dry?

Residents living on a floodplain often have little or no chance to prepare for a downpour. But the flood-resistant fort we created for the Irish town of Mallow has transformed the lives of local people.

For centuries, residents in this area of County Cork have been at the mercy of the River Blackwater. In recent decades, its 12,000 inhabitants have had to batten down the hatches at least every three to four years as waters flooded the main commercial street in the town, regularly causing considerable damage to local businesses.

In 2003 we were commissioned by Ireland's Office of Public Works to carry out a study of potential flood-relief measures for the town. After a detailed assessment, we suggested defending Mallow with a combination of defence walls, moveable barriers that can be raised between permanent structures, flood-relief culverts designed to divert water, and the lowering of the floodplain at the town's main bridge. The first completed stage of the work was put to the test in November 2009.

When significant flooding was forecast, residents and businesspeople stayed in the town centre to witness the flood barriers lifting as 1.5m of water surged against the other side. It became a carnival-style event, with shops staying open late and people watching – none of them got wet. It is proof that a bit of careful planning can help keep an entire town dry.

**Project name:** Munster Blackwater River (Mallow) Flood Relief Scheme
**Designed for:** Office of Public Works
**Designed with:** McGinty & O'Shea

Defending the town of Mallow: our solution consists of defence walls, moveable barriers and flood-relief culverts

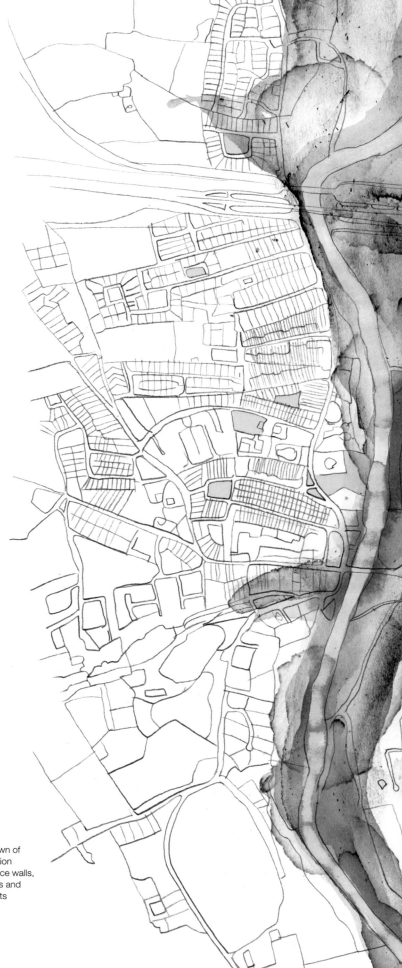

# Rising tides? Lessons from King Canute

As King Canute proved, even kings cannot hold back the sea – but a new approach could forever change the way we tackle flooding. In Yorkshire, the Humber Estuary has become a focal point for testing ways to reduce the impact of rising sea levels.

There, we worked with the UK Environment Agency on a plan that will help drive their work over the next 100 years. Part of the plan is the 'managed realignment' of the estuarine defences in some locations. This means deliberately breaching or even removing sea walls and embankments so flood water can flow into former floodplains, creating new intertidal habitats, including saltmarsh, mudflats and saline lagoons.

One aspect of our work has involved developing a framework for evaluating the economic benefits created by these new habitats. These benefits include carbon capture, pollution control and acting as nurseries for young fish. They can also reduce the risk of erosion and absorb wave energy, so that our coastlines are more resilient.

What started as a small study can now be rolled out nationally; it's not stopping the tides, but it is moving them so water goes to the right places.

**Project name:** Humber Estuary, ecosystem services valuation framework
**Designed for:** Environment Agency

# Shigeru Ban

## Natural disasters can bring out the best in design

There is an inherent tension in the work architects do. While we are able to create beautiful, useful and innovative buildings, we are often guilty of not working for the benefit of society, but instead for rich people, governments and developers. These clients often have noble goals, but they may hire us to create something that reflects their power and money, rather than give back to society.

And yet, architects' solutions can make a huge difference in society. One area in particular – which may seem unusual given the chaos they cause – is when natural disasters occur. In the aftermath of earthquakes, communities need the specialist skills of architects to construct the best temporary housing.

It is vital for temporary housing to be both cost-effective and recyclable. With this in mind, I became the only architect in the world to make buildings out of paper tubes. After using them for the first time in 1986, I have built temporary housing this way following earthquakes and other refugee crises in countries as far apart as China, Turkey, Italy and Rwanda. It is a solution that works because the material is much stronger than you may expect and can be made waterproof and fireproof.

Paper can do more than simply provide temporary accommodation. It can also provide basic human dignity when disaster strips these rights away. The 2011 earthquake and subsequent tsunami off the east coast of Japan devastated huge numbers of lives and caused the greatest humanitarian crisis in the country since the Second World War. In the weeks and months following the disaster, tens of thousands of people who had lost their homes were forced to live in evacuation centres set up by the government, such as gymnasiums. This often left families without even the most basic levels of privacy.

In these kinds of situations, it is vital to be able to think creatively to come up with solutions. Our paper partition system provides cost-effective, easy-to-assemble privacy for families who have been evacuated from their homes. We installed more than 1,800 units of the system, which creates temporary privacy through a combination of paper tubes and canvas curtains, in over 50 evacuation centres.

It makes you wonder what exactly we mean when we say that a building is temporary or permanent. Any building can be destroyed if another developer buys the land and wants something new. But a temporary church we built after the 1995 Kobe earthquake was later donated to Taiwan and is still in use. It proves that even a paper building can become permanent if people love it.

**Shigeru Ban** is a Japanese architect known for his innovative work with paper

"It is vital for
temporary housing to
be both cost- effective
and recyclable"

How do you
help rebuild
lives after a
tsunami?

Using shipping containers as temporary housing in the aftermath of a natural disaster has been done before. But when the 2011 tsunami and earthquake devastated Japan's coastline, leaving many of the residents of the town of Onagawa-cho homeless, it also left limited flatland above the tsunami zone, and that meant limited space, even for shipping containers.

Our approach – working with a disaster relief housing specialist – was to find a way to stack the containers and create multi-storey accommodation.

Our response called on work we had done on a previous project. Then, we had found that, by building a lattice of standard containers and frames, housing blocks could be created that were both resistant to seismic disturbances and better insulated for sound, damp and heat than their wooden counterparts. Better still, once residents could return to their old homes, the containers could be disassembled and reused as immediate disaster relief or as a simple shipping container.

So far, so good. But one challenge remained. Japan's temporary homes, built by the government's Prefabrication Housing Association, are typically single-storey and often wooden, requiring a large ground footprint and the labour to construct them. We helped secure the local mayor's approval for the project – and then the work began. A 60-container block could be assembled in a single day, and within 12 weeks 189 housing units were ready for the Onagawa community.

Today the residents are so settled that many of them now joke that their temporary homes are finished to a higher standard than their former houses.

**Project name:** Multi-storey Container Temporary Housing
**Designed for:** Town of Onagawa-cho
**Designed with:** Shigeru Ban Architects

"We didn't really know if the housing would be comfortable to live in until it was completed, but I have heard from people who live there and they are glad they waited"

**Nobutaka Azumi, former mayor of Onagawa town**

Will a 21st-century skyscraper redefine our skylines?

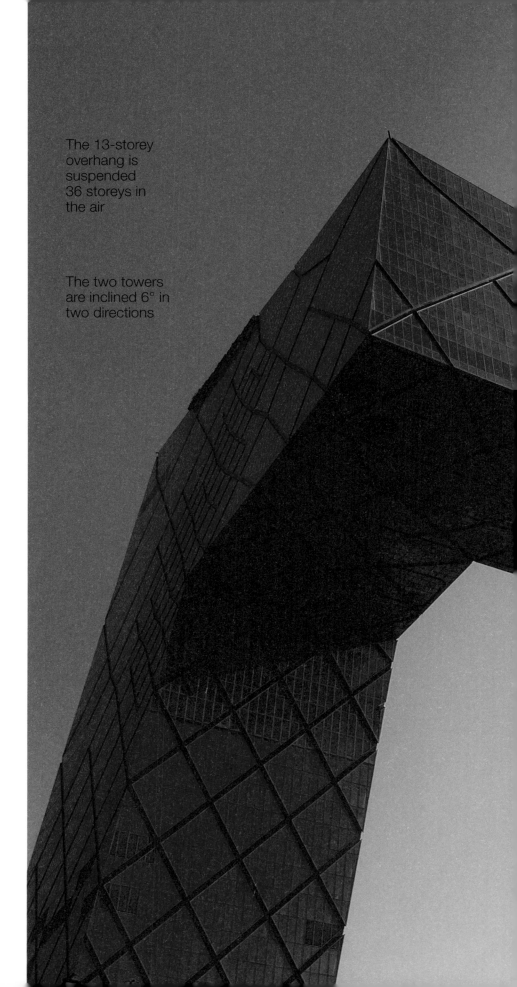

The 13-storey overhang is suspended 36 storeys in the air

The two towers are inclined 6° in two directions

For almost a century, skyscraper design has been about building them tall. But when the Chinese city of Beijing sought a contemporary architectural icon, they rewrote the rules.

The CCTV Building, the headquarters for China Central Television, may be just 51 storeys high, but there is no other building like it. Affectionately known as 'the big pants', it is formed of two connected, leaning towers that form a continuous loop.

Redefining the skyscraper was never going to be about easy design. As a working television station, China Central Television had very specific requirements about using internal space to encourage communication. The architect devised the looping form to encourage CCTV staff to mingle, reducing the compartmentalised 'ghettos' that can develop during the TV production process.

The form of the CCTV Building provides a single loop of interconnected activities around a 9-storey 'base', two leaning 'towers' that slope inwards at 6° in two directions, and a 13-storey 'overhang', suspended 36 storeys high in the air and cantilevering 75m from its supports.

Our engineering designers first had to ensure that this 3D, looping form was structurally feasible. With a global team working between London, Hong Kong and Beijing, we analysed the construction stage

The building's steel bracing is densest in the areas that require most support

by stage. Getting it built was only part of the challenge: it is located in a seismic zone, which means it had to withstand potential earthquake activity, both when completed and during the build.

The building is supported by a grid-like tubular exoskeleton. The areas that are under highest stress have the densest diagonal pattern of steel bracing, allowing passers-by to visualise the flow of force around the form.

The two towers were constructed separately and the overhang sections were gradually launched outwards from each. Weather conditions were a significant factor as the connection became imminent, since the independent structures would both expand in the heat and sway in the wind. It meant the joining process had to happen quickly in the cool early morning before the heat of the sun started to warm the steel skeleton, to prevent the risk of overstressing the key connection pieces.

It's a world landmark and a building that takes skyscraper design, structure and construction to a new level.

**Project name:** China Central Television (CCTV) Headquarters
**Designed for:** CCTV
**Designed with:** OMA (Rem Koolhaas & Ole Scheeren) with East China Architectural Design & Research Institute

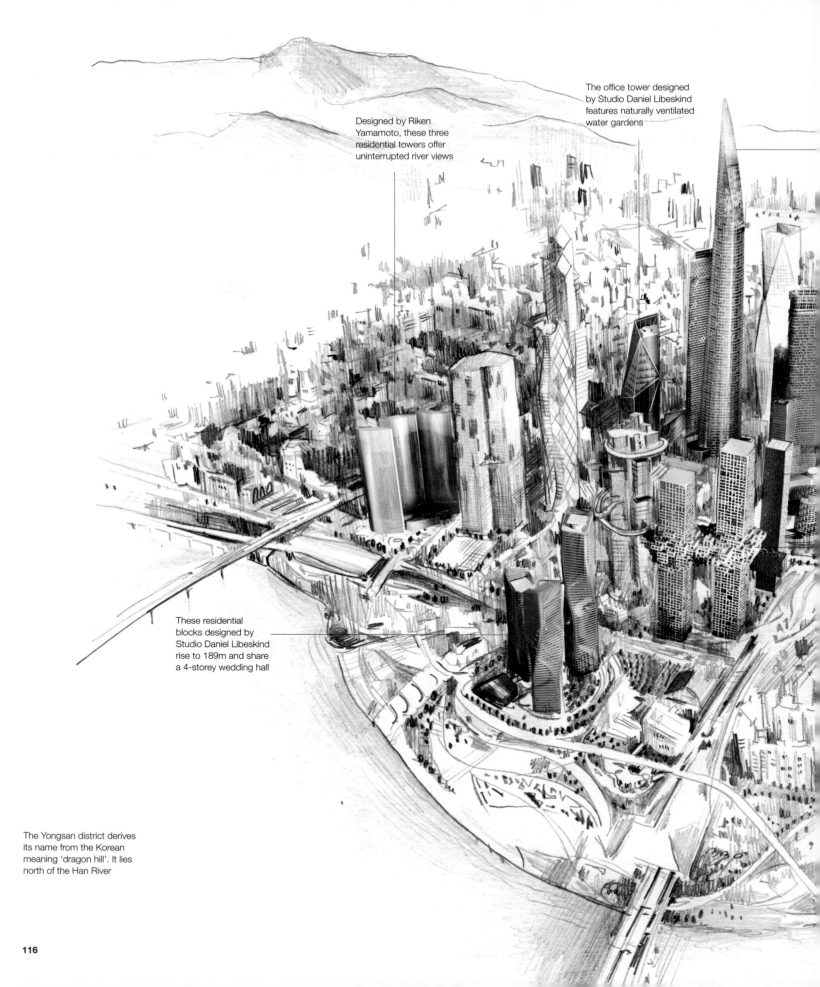

The office tower designed by Studio Daniel Libeskind features naturally ventilated water gardens

Designed by Riken Yamamoto, these three residential towers offer uninterrupted river views

These residential blocks designed by Studio Daniel Libeskind rise to 189m and share a 4-storey wedding hall

The Yongsan district derives its name from the Korean meaning 'dragon hill'. It lies north of the Han River

The centrepiece of the development will be Renzo Piano's 620m Landmark Tower

The hotel tower designed by KPF features spectacular views of the Han River to the south and the rugged mountains to the north

Residential buildings designed by Asymptote Architecture and BIG complete the Yongsan residential precinct

These two residential blocks designed by MVRDV are connected by a 10-storey 'cloud'

# Teamwork makes the dream work, doesn't it?

Our global teams have come together to help create a collection of the world's most ambitious skyscrapers in the South Korean capital, Seoul.

Working on eight cutting-edge buildings gave us the opportunity to pool our expertise internationally, creating a collaborative approach. Our involvement began when we worked on the masterplan for the 3.4 million square metre scheme in the initial phase, to work out how best to develop the waterside location.

Today our work includes the centrepiece of the new development – the Renzo Piano Building Workshop's 620m-high Landmark Tower – a pair of residential blocks connected by a 10-storey 'cloud', and other hotel, residential and office buildings.

Our design teams wanted a united approach; one that ensured we pooled the best of all our skills and got the best results through sharing and collaboration. In the process we learned much from each other.

The vision will start to come to life in 2016; by then our designers will be able to see how teamwork has inspired a new business district.

**Project name:** Archipelago 21: Landmark Tower ( Site B1-1), Site H1, Site R7, Site B2-1, Site R1, Site R2, Site R4a, Site R4b
**Designed for:** Dreamhub (owner), Studio Daniel Libeskind (masterplan architect)
**Designed with:** Renzo Piano Building Workshop, Samoo Architects & Engineers, Kohn Pedersen Fox Associates (KPF), Asymptote Architecture, SIAPLAN Architects & Planners, Studio Daniel Libeskind, Mooyoung Architects & Engineers, Riken Yamamoto & Field Shop, Haeahn Architecture, MVRDV, Bjarke Ingels Group (BIG)

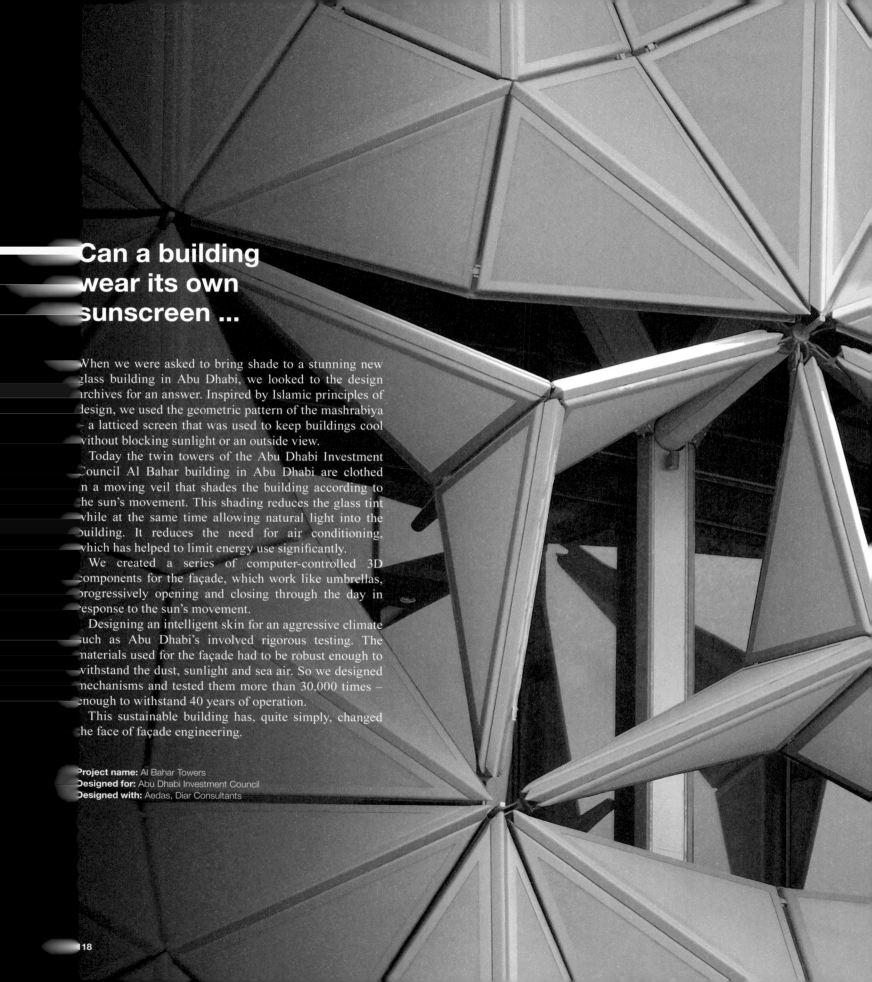

# Can a building wear its own sunscreen ...

When we were asked to bring shade to a stunning new glass building in Abu Dhabi, we looked to the design archives for an answer. Inspired by Islamic principles of design, we used the geometric pattern of the mashrabiya – a latticed screen that was used to keep buildings cool without blocking sunlight or an outside view.

Today the twin towers of the Abu Dhabi Investment Council Al Bahar building in Abu Dhabi are clothed in a moving veil that shades the building according to the sun's movement. This shading reduces the glass tint while at the same time allowing natural light into the building. It reduces the need for air conditioning, which has helped to limit energy use significantly.

We created a series of computer-controlled 3D components for the façade, which work like umbrellas, progressively opening and closing through the day in response to the sun's movement.

Designing an intelligent skin for an aggressive climate such as Abu Dhabi's involved rigorous testing. The materials used for the façade had to be robust enough to withstand the dust, sunlight and sea air. So we designed mechanisms and tested them more than 30,000 times – enough to withstand 40 years of operation.

This sustainable building has, quite simply, changed the face of façade engineering.

Project name: Al Bahar Towers
Designed for: Abu Dhabi Investment Council
Designed with: Aedas, Diar Consultants

# ... and can a greenhouse stop getting too hot?

Using the right type of glass means the stunning domes at Singapore's Gardens by the Bay let light in but keep heat out. The Flower Dome and Cloud Forest are home to 250,000 species of plants and operate as climate-controlled conservatories. The glazing and geometry of each had to be designed to deliver precise climatic performance.

To protect the plants and combat very bright days, there is a light-sensitive shading system, with sails that unfurl from the steel arches of the structure and are completely hidden when not in use. Electronically controlled vents allow air out when it is too hot, and would allow smoke to vent in the event of a fire.

Each conservatory is made up of thousands of glass panels: they give a great view of Marina Bay from the inside and of thousands of plants from the outside. But different sizes and shapes of panel had to be created to fit in the dome-shaped design. Through a detailed computer optimisation we used just 42 different sizes of glass panel on the 3,332-panel Flower Dome and 690 different sizes on the 2,577-panel Cloud Forest, simplifying the creation, construction and maintenance of the glazing.

**Project name:** Gardens by the Bay
**Designed for:** CPG Consultants Pte Ltd, NParks
**Designed with:** Wilkinson Eyre Architects

# Can a building float?

Visitors to the Stedelijk Museum in Amsterdam could be forgiven for thinking they are hallucinating. The new extension to the historic building looks like a giant bathtub and seems to float above the ground.

As structural engineers, we were instrumental in delivering a triumphant combination of the old and the new. The modern bathtub-shaped extension is held up by five columns and a concrete wall; but the majestic original building is visible through the ground floor's glass façade.

To complement the exterior, we designed lighting that allows the maximum amount of daylight in without damaging the artwork on show. It's a good example of art being on the inside – and the outside.

**Project name:** Stedelijk Museum
**Designed for:** City of Amsterdam
**Designed with:** Benthem Crouwel Architects

# A stone that makes waves

# Impossible?

# Not in Sydney

Transforming an artist's vision from a small clay model into a 350-tonne sculpture in the heart of Sydney's Royal Botanic Gardens was no mean feat. But we brought Chris Booth's ambitious Wurrungwuri sculpture to life using 3D digital modelling.

From guiding the quarry's computerised diamond-wire saw and cutting sandstone blocks to size, through to testing the highly intricate build process, every step was informed by a 3D digital reference model.

The result is the city's most expensive sculpture, Wurrungwuri. The name means 'this side of the water' – and the sculpture's wave form reflects this. A 13m wave made from 250 blocks of Sydney's famous Hawkesbury sandstone, it echoes the geological history of nearby Farm Cove.

The artist was thrilled to see his idea realised. And it has been embraced by the local community as a landmark; is loved by children, who can clamber over it; and is lived in by plants, insects and birds, which have found their way into the gaps in the sculpture.

**Project name:** Wurrungwuri
**Designed for:** Sydney Royal Botanic Gardens & Domain Trust, The Johnson Estate
**Designed with:** Chris Booth, Gosford Quarries, The Traditional Restoration Company

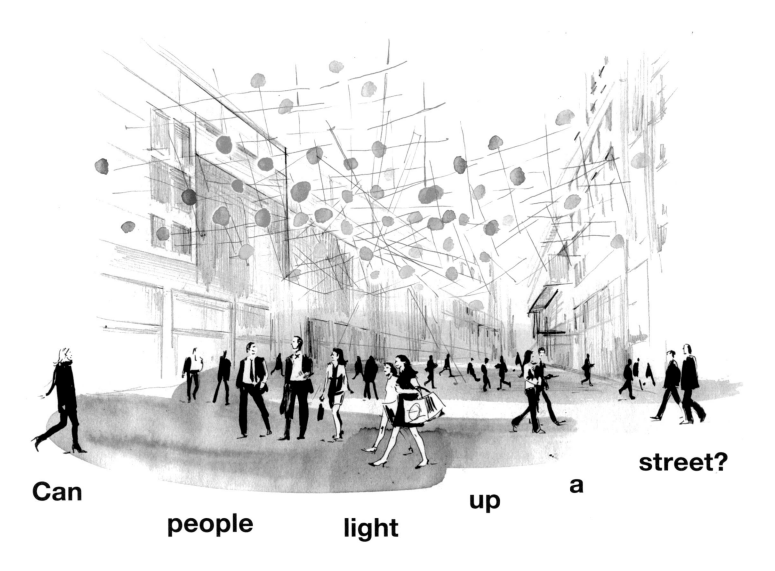

# Can people light up a street?

Your smile might be able to light up a room, but how about your body illuminating a street? Our lighting designers have created lights that become brighter the more people walk beneath them. It is part of a wider project to draw shoppers to the Grote Marktstraat shopping street in The Hague, Netherlands.

The interactive light installations, which are positioned at the street's three main junctions, will be fitted with cameras that change according to the speed, direction and number of shoppers walking below. The lights will change colour depending on the flow of people below, so the street will look different on busy and quiet days.

To make the light 'struts' look as if they're floating, we created a 'tensegrity' structure. This network of cables creates a geometry with such tension that it can keep the struts in place without any two of them touching.

Designed as part of the complete redevelopment of the Grote Marktstraat area – including buildings, pavements and furniture – these striking interactive lights will brighten up the city's streets.

**Project name:** Redevelopment Grote Marktstraat, The Hague
**Designed for:** City of The Hague
**Designed with:** ELV architecten

# It's 40°C and the mercury is still rising. Can you stay cool?

The answer can be found at 1 Bligh Street in Sydney. There, a striking 27-level office building, with its elliptical shape and 139m-high naturally ventilated atrium, has raised the bar for premium sustainable high-rise office space in Australia.

Office workers get great harbour views, but the building combines style and substance. Its double-skin façade features automated blinds that adapt to the sun's path, allowing optimal temperature and light control. It is a solution that will help address the global issue of rising temperatures – and in Sydney it can reach peaks of 40°C.

This built-in solar control means occupants stay cool while looking out of clearer glass than is generally used in a commercial building. The building is flooded with natural light; almost three-quarters of the building is within 8m of either the façade or the internal atrium.

The show-stopping central atrium features a sophisticated louvered ventilation system that allows fresh air into the offices while serving as a smoke-control system in the event of a fire. The building also has an energy-efficient hybrid air-conditioning system, a solar-powered cooling system and toilets that use recycled mains water.

1 Bligh Street is proof that sustainability and innovation do not need to compromise comfort.

**Project name:** 1 Bligh Street, Sydney
**Designed for:** DEXUS Property Group, DEXUS Wholesale Property Fund, Cbus Property
**Designed with:** Architectus in association with ingenhoven

# Credits

In alphabetical order

**1 Bligh Street, Sydney, Australia, p124**
Photography: Lon Fong Martin / Getty (smaller image)
Main photography: DEXUS Funds Management Limited
(external); photo credit: 1 Bligh is owned and managed
by DEXUS, DWPF and Cbus Property

**Accident Fund Insurance Company Headquarters,
US, p22**
Illustration: Elisabeth Moch / YCN; photography:
Ian Buckley / Manochie Photography

**Al Bahar Towers, UAE, p118**
Photography: courtesy of Arup

**AQ2 and A Rita Water Pipeline, Philippines, p89**
Photography: Jon Fabrigar / Xinhua Press / Corbis

**Archipelago 21: Landmark Tower (Site B1-1), Site H1,
Site R7, Site B2-1, Site R1, Site R2, Site R4a, Site R4b,
South Korea, p116**
Illustration: Elizabeth Moch / YCN; CGI art: Charlie Rabicano

**Arup Inspect, p29**
Illustration: Raymond Biesinger

**Boston Manor Viaduct, UK, p40**
Photography: Getty

**Bradford City Park, UK, p48**
Photography: Mark Davis

**Brisbane Airport Link, Australia, p52**
Photography: courtesy of Arup

**Cairns Botanic Gardens Visitor Centre, Australia, p10**
Photography: Patrick Bingham-Hall / Pesaro Publishing

**California High-Speed Rail Plan, US, p56**
Illustration: Ciara Phelan / YCN

**Center for the Arts at Virginia Tech, US, p75**
Photography: Don Farrall / Getty

**Channel Tunnel Rail Link, Stratford City, London
Olympic and Paralympic Games, HDTV sport lighting,
UK, p14**
Photography: Jason Hawkes, Manuel Gutjahr / Getty, PCN
Photography / Alamy, Diane Auckland / Arcaid / Corbis,
Development Securities PLC & Realstar Group

**China Central Television (CCTV) Headquarters,
China, p112**
Photography: Frederic J Brown / Getty, Emanuele
Ciccomartino / Robert Harding World Imagery / Corbis

**Climate Action in Megacities: C40 Cities Baseline and
Opportunities, p54**
Photography: Johanna Ward / Wardour

**COFCO Agricultural Eco Valley, China, p90**
Illustration: Anna Garforth

**East La Mesa Water Treatment Plant, Philippines, p88**
Photography: Jon Fabrigar / Xinhua Press / Corbis

**East River Waterfront Esplanade, US, p66**
Cover illustration: Elisabeth Moch / YCN; photography:
Adam Golfer

**Engineering Building, National University of Ireland,
Galway, Ireland, p42**
Photography: Johanna Ward / Wardour

**Feasibility studies for a proposed Linear Collider, p24**
Photography: Denis Balibouse / Corbis

**Gardens by the Bay, Singapore, p119**
Photography: Darren Soh, courtesy of Arup

**Gerald Desmond Bridge Replacement Project,
US, p84**
Illustration: Oli Frape; photography: courtesy of Arup

**GRAVITAS Offshore concrete gravity foundation, p50**
Illustration: Elisabeth Moch / YCN

**HKIA Midfield Development, Hong Kong, p57**

**Humber Estuary, ecosystem, UK, p107**
Illustration: Elizabeth Moch / YCN

**Innovation Oakland, US, p59**
Illustration: Raymond Biesinger

**Kadare Cultural Centre, Japan, p76**
Photography: Sergio Pirrone

**Lloyd's Cloudless, UK, p4**
Photography: Sean McGarr / Flickr / Getty, Johanna Ward
/ Wardour

**Lou Reed's Metal Machine Trio, US, p20**
Photography: Neal Preston / Corbis, Dave Rife, courtesy
of Arup

**Low Energy Lighting Guide for TV
Productions, UK, p51**
Photography: Pixeleyes Photography

**Metropol Parasol, Plaza de la Encarnación, Spain, p38**
Photography: David Franck, Tim E White / Cultura
Travel / Getty

**MOPT Stormwater Harvesting Scheme, Australia, p102**
Photography: epa european pressphoto agency b.v. / Alamy

The Arup Design Book is produced and published
for Arup by Wardour

**For Arup**
Arup Design Book Publishing Board
Tristram Carfrae, Malcolm Smith, Duncan Wilkinson

Piers van Til, Creative Director
Renée McTavish, Project Director
Victoria Maunder, Project Manager

**For Wardour**
The core team was led by Claire Oldfield who also took
the editorial lead, and Ben Barrett, who took the creative
lead. The team included: designers Jenni Dennis and
Lynn Jones, picture researcher Johanna Ward, editor
James Cash and project managers Georgina Beach
and Paula Beardsley.

Thanks to the writers, editors, researchers and artworkers
who worked alongside the core team and with the wider
production team – there are too many to mention.

Wardour, Drury House, 34-43 Russell Street,
London WC2B 5HA, United Kingdom
+44 (0)20 7010 0999
www.wardour.co.uk

Arup Design Book is printed
by DeckersSnoeck, Antwerp
on FSC certified material.

Arup Design Book
50 design questions answered
ISBN no: 978-0953823949

Trade Distribution: Marston Book Services (UK), Ingram
Publisher Services (USA), Woodslane Pty Ltd. (Australia)
and Titles (South Africa).

Also available direct from Harriman House
(www.harriman-house.com) and all good bookshops.
£30/$50

This book is also available as an iTunes app.

# ARUP